Keto Diet Cookbook for]

+

Keto Diet for Women Over 60

2 BOOKS IN 1

A Complete Guide to Learn Why It Is Never Too Late to Live the Keto Lifestyle

- Quick and Tasty Low-Carb Recipes, 2 Meal Plans & Shopping List Included -

By

Melinda Francis

Table of Contents

KETO DIET COOKBOOK FOR BEGINNERS

Introduction

The ketogenic diet aims to encourage your body to burn fat for energy by substituting relatively few carbs with fat. Two health advantages are losing weight and reducing your chance of contracting certain illnesses. A high-fat diet known as the ketogenic diet may help certain epileptics, particularly young children. It is not a miracle treatment, but it is one option for the different anti-epileptic drugs on the market. For certain kids, better seizure control and, in other situations, increased mental alertness are benefits of the ketogenic diet that may be achieved with fewer drugs. The keto diet is sometimes considered a challenging regimen to adhere to. Still, with experience and knowledge of what it strives to accomplish, it can be made into a workable schedule. The main goal is to replace carbs like sugar and bread as the body's main fuel source with fats. To achieve this, one must consume much less carbs while increasing their consumption of fats. The diet is so stringent that all items consumed must be measured down to a 1/10 of a gram throughout meal preparation, and participants are not allowed to consume anything that has not been "approved" by the dietician. The quantity of carbs permitted is so minimal that even the little sugar in most liquid or chewable medicines will make the diet ineffective. For example, a typical dinner may consist of a certain sort of meat and green vegetables cooked with a lot of butter or mayonnaise. For sipping, heavy cream could be added on the side. Another dish can have eggs and bacon with plenty of oil or butter and heavy cream. For food to be effective, an extremely large proportion of fats to carbs must be preserved with a low consumption of total calories. A ketogenic diet could be an alternative for some individuals who have had trouble reducing weight with conventional techniques. Depending on each person's genetic make-up and body composition, different amounts of fat, carbohydrates, and protein are required to attain certain health advantages. Therefore, if someone decides to commence a ketogenic diet, they should speak with their doctor and a dietitian to generate a meal plan customized to their current health conditions, stop nutritional deficiencies, and thoroughly monitor any biochemical changes after beginning the regimen. When resuming carbs after weight reduction, a dietician may also provide advice.

Chapter 1: What is Keto Diet?

A Keto diet is intended to induce ketosis, which causes body fat to break down, making ketones, enabling the body to operate majorly on ketones despite glucose. Several techniques are available to induce ketosis; thus, the ketogenic diet has numerous variations. The numerous varieties of ketogenic diets often have multiple characteristics since the ultimate result of such diets is similar, particularly in becoming high in dietary fat and low in carbohydrates.

What is Ketosis?

A keto diet aims to induce what is known as a ketosis or ketogenic state. A metabolic state known as ketosis generates substances known as ketone bodies to replace glucose as the main energy source for the central nervous system and the brain. When you eat insufficient carbohydrates, and your body runs out of glycogen and glucose, you enter ketosis. When your body runs out of carbohydrates, it resorts to burning fat as energy and produces ketones. You should ideally start to enter ketosis a few days into the keto diet. Kits are available to test your urine and blood for ketones and determine if you're in ketosis. During the initial two weeks of beginning the keto diet, some individuals suffer the keto flu. Unlike the flu, this is not a genuine infection. Instead, it's a collection of signs that resemble the flu. Although the cause of the keto flu in some individuals is unknown, it may be connected to how successfully a person's metabolism adapts to utilizing fat instead of carbohydrates as its main fuel source.

The following are possible keto flu symptoms:

- Headache

- Chills and fever

- Problems sleeping

- Sugar cravings

- Fatigue

- Nausea, diarrhea, vomiting, and constipation

- Trouble concentrating, confusion, and irritability

- Stomach pain

1.1   Different types of Keto Diets

Following are the basic types of the Keto diet.

SKD - Standard Ketogenic Diet

Regards to grams each day, a typical conventional ketogenic diet is a moderate protein, very low carb, and high-fat diet, generally including 20 percent protein, 70 to 75 percent fat, and around 5 to 10 percent carbohydrates.

- 40 to 60g of protein

- 20 to 50g of the carbohydrate

- Fat of no limit

To be considered the ketogenic diet, all fat must make up the bulk of your calories. There is no cap since everyone's needs for energy might differ greatly. Vegetables should play a significant role in ketogenic diets, majorly non-starchy veggies, since they contain very low carbohydrate content. Standard ketogenic diet (SKD) has repeatedly shown their ability to help patients lose weight, manage the blood sugar levels, and enhance their cardiovascular health.

WFKD - Well-Formulated Ketogenic Diet

One of the foremost experts regarding ketogenic diets, Steve Phinney, coined the phrase well-formulated keto diet. WFKD adheres to a similar structure to the conventional ketogenic diet. When the ratios of protein, macronutrients, fat, and carbohydrate are met, the diet is said to be well-formulated, increasing the likelihood of ketosis.

Calorie-restricted ketogenic diet

A calorie-restricted ketogenic diet is identical to a regular ketogenic diet, except the amount of calories is capped at a certain number. According to research, ketogenic diets are often effective if or not calorie intake is controlled. It is because consuming fat while remaining in a state of ketosis has a satiating impact that tends to assist avoids overeating.

TKD - Targeted Ketogenic Diet

TKD is comparable to a typical ketogenic diet despite carbs are consumed just after and before workouts. This is a middle ground between a cyclical and a traditional ketogenic diet which permits you to eat carbs any day you go to the gym. It relies on the concept that since our muscles need more energy while we are active, carbohydrates ingested after or before an exertion will be absorbed much more effectively.

VLCKD - Very-low-carb ketogenic diet

A VLCKD often refers to a normal ketogenic diet since it is extremely low in carbohydrates.

Ketogenic Diet MCT

It adheres to the general principles of the ketogenic diet yet focuses on employing MCTs (medium-chain triglycerides) to give most of the diet's fat. Coconut oil contains MCTs, also present in MCT emulsion drinks and MCT oil. Due to the idea that MCTs enable patients to consume more protein and carbs in ketosis, MCT ketogenic diets have been treated as used to treat epilepsy. Long-chain triglycerides found in typical dietary fat, as opposed to MCTs, give more ketones for every fat gram. Be aware that consuming MCTs alone might cause nausea and diarrhea. Eating meals having an addition of non-MCT and MCT fat is preferable to avoid this. However, studies examining whether MCTs have broader advantages for weight reduction or sugar blood levels are lacking.

CKD - Cyclical Ketogenic Diet

In a CKD diet, commonly known as carb backloading, days with increased carbohydrate intake are included, like 5 ketogenic days accompanied by two days with higher carb intake. This diet is designed for athletes to utilize the days of having more carbohydrates to replace muscle glycogen depleted after exercise.

High Protein Ketogenic Diet

With a ratio of 60% fat, 35% protein, and 5% carbohydrates, this diet has greater protein than a normal ketogenic diet. According to research, a protein-high keto diet may help those who want to reduce weight. There isn't enough information to say if a long-term ketogenic diet has any health hazards similar to other ketogenic diets.

1.2   Proven Benefits of a Ketogenic Diet

The following are a few purported health advantages of the keto diet:

- **Improve cholesterol levels**

The "bad" cholesterol, low-density lipoproteins (LDL), is more prone to result in plaque and heart disease. The "good" cholesterol, high-density lipoproteins (HDL), is known for reducing the chance of developing heart disease. According to research, adopting a ketogenic diet may help lower total cholesterol while raising HDL levels. As a result, the keto diet could decrease your risk of heart disease by lowering cholesterol.

- **Improve blood sugar control and insulin resistance**

Our cells absorb glucose from the carbs we consume thanks to the hormone insulin. An ability to resist insulin may result in persistently elevated blood sugar, which over time, may progress to type 2 diabetes. People have looked to low-carbohydrate diets as a potential means of controlling their glucose levels since high blood glucose levels characterize diabetes. According to research, type 2 diabetics who follow the ketogenic diet may have better insulin sensitivity and blood sugar regulation. When you're diagnosed with diabetes and are taking medication, it's crucial to discuss any dietary changes you're thinking about making with your doctor since your medicines may need to be monitored more carefully.

- **Encourage weight loss**

The keto diet's purported advantages for weight reduction are one of many common reasons individuals try it. Several studies show that a ketogenic diet is superior to a low-fat diet for quick, short-term weight reduction. But a significant portion of the starting weight reduction could have been water weight. According to some studies, the keto diet could be superior to other eating regimens in terms of reducing belly body fat and promoting long-term weight reduction. Because it covers the organs, visceral fat is another name for abdominal fat. This fat raises the chance of developing chronic conditions, including diabetes, fatty liver, and heart disease.

- **Reduces seizures**

Before anti-seizure drugs were often utilized, the ketogenic diet initially emerged to prevent seizures. The ketogenic diet remains used today to treat those who struggle to manage their seizures using medication alone.

- **Lower blood pressure**

Chronic renal disease, stroke, and heart disease are more likely to develop in those with persistently high blood pressure. According to research, eating a ketogenic diet may help decrease blood pressure and keep it healthy.

Health conditions that may benefit from a keto diet

Following a ketogenic diet may be advantageous for several medical issues, including:

Prediabetes and diabetes

Insulin resistance is a prevalent characteristic of prediabetes and type 2 diabetes. According to studies, the keto diet may increase insulin sensitivity, and sticking to a keto meal plan may improve blood sugar management. According to some studies, the ketogenic diet may even be useful in curing type 2 diabetes and may minimize the quantity of diabetic medication required.

Heart disease

Heart disorders, including heart attacks, coronary artery disease, and stroke, are more likely to affect those with excessive cholesterol and uncontrolled high blood pressure. A ketogenic diet may help enhance heart health by managing these risk factors.

Neurodegenerative diseases

Ketosis may be beneficial for treating neurological and brain diseases, including Parkinson's and Alzheimer's. According to preliminary studies, a ketogenic diet could assist in lessening the symptoms of several of these diseases. Although the exact process is unclear, it is thought that ketone bodies may contribute to preserving the health of the neurons and nerves affected by various illnesses. In turn, safeguarding the neurons and nerves may aid in delaying the aging process in the brain.

Epilepsy

People with epilepsy may benefit from practicing the keto diet, as its initial goal was to help control seizures.

It works best for patients whose seizures are difficult to control with antiepileptic drugs.

Heart health

A low-carb diet, however, may raise the likelihood of low blood sugar if you use diabetic drugs. If you have diabetes, be cautious to consult your doctor before beginning a low-carb diet.

Metabolic syndrome

Heart attacks, strokes, and other chronic illnesses are all at an increased risk due to a combination of symptoms known as metabolic syndrome. There aren't many symptoms in the early stages of metabolic syndrome. Still, it accumulates over time and raises your chance of more severe illnesses and bad cardiovascular health. The following five conditions make up metabolic syndrome:

- High blood pressure

- Excess fat around the waist

- High cholesterol

- High blood sugar

- High triglycerides

According to some studies, these illnesses may benefit from a ketogenic diet.

1.3   Contraindications and Risks of the Keto Diet

When starting this diet, people with diabetes receiving oral hypoglycemic medicines or insulin risk developing severe hypoglycemia if their medications are not properly adjusted. Patients with liver disease, pancreatitis, and problems with fat metabolism, carnitine palmitoyltransferase deficiency, primary carnitine deficit, carnitine translocase deficiency, pyruvate kinase deficiency, or porphyrias should not follow the ketogenic diet. Rarely may a ketogenic diet cause an error breath test for alcohol. Hepatic alcohol dehydrogenase may sometimes convert acetone in the body to isopropanol due to ketonemia, which can result in an error alcohol breath test outcome. The most frequent and often mild short-term adverse effects caused by the ketogenic diet are a slew of symptoms frequently referred to as the "keto flu": vomiting, nausea, headaches, lethargy, dizziness, and sleeplessness. Within a few days to a few weeks, these symptoms go away. Ensuring enough fluids and electrolytes might help reduce some of these symptoms.

Hepatic steatosis, kidney stones, hypoproteinemia, and mineral and vitamin shortages are some of the long-term negative consequences.

1.4 Keto Diet Tips: Go Keto in 5 Steps

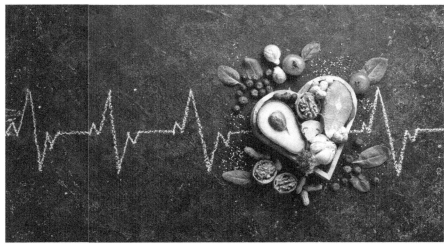

To increase your success, adhere to these five steps.

- **Before you begin the keto diet, decide what your health objectives are.**

What are your intentions for beginning the keto diet, and how would you evaluate your progress? You could want to lose weight, or you might also want to improve other aspects of your health, including reducing your blood sugar. Early goal-setting will keep you motivated and reduce drawbacks.

The condition diabetes. To reduce your blood sugar, you could opt for the keto diet. Before beginning this strategy, discuss with your doctor if you use diabetic medication. Hypoglycemia, sometimes known as low blood sugar, may be harmful. To prevent low blood sugar, your doctor may advise that you take less diabetic medication. Once you begin a ketogenic diet, you might have to check your blood sugar level more often and adjust your medication if it falls too low.

Determining whether to monitor ketones. To determine whether you have been in ketosis and to adjust your carbohydrate target, you may decide to check your ketone levels. Breath, urine, and blood may all be seen.

If your blood pressure or cholesterol is high. When you begin a ketogenic diet, the blood cholesterol levels might remain unchanged, but they do rise noticeably for some individuals. Ask your doctor if you ought to get your cholesterol level or other laboratory tests checked after beginning the diet.

Additionally, if you are taking blood pressure medication, discussing it with your doctor is crucial. Any diet plan that results in significant weight reduction may reduce blood pressure. Even though this is a positive diet outcome, you may need to reduce your blood pressure medication to prevent your blood pressure from falling too low.

- **Establish dietary goals**

Targeting proteins. Keto diets provide a modest amount of protein—around 20% of calories. While consuming adequate protein to prevent muscle loss is necessary, excessive protein intake should be avoided. Since your body can produce glucose from protein, a high-protein diet may prevent you from entering ketosis.

Goal carbs. You may choose a percent carb goal, typically 5 to 10%, or a carb gram goal to tailor your carbohydrate aim. Many ketogenic diet programs start with 20 to 30 grams of "net carb" daily. Total carbs less fiber equals net carbs. For instance, 12 almonds offer two grams of fiber and around 3 grams of total carbohydrates. To obtain one gram of net carb, subtract 2 grams of fiber from the 3 grams of total carbs. You may increase the amount of nutritious nuts, veggies, and seeds in your diet by tracking net carbs.

- **Fill up your kitchen.**

When you begin a ketogenic diet, you can feel as if eating habits have been completely flipped upside-down. Spend some time making plans for your new way of life. Keep any enticing high-carb meals out of the kitchen to remain on track. You may also boost your success by stocking your kitchen with foods suitable for the keto diet.

Popular keto-friendly meals are listed below:

Vegetables. Leafy green vegetables, including spinach, kale, and lettuce, are extremely low in carbohydrates and contain vitamins and minerals. Low-carb vegetables may be consumed in moderation, including asparagus, broccoli, bell peppers, zucchini, and cauliflower.

Protein-Rich Meats and Foods. You can eat tofu, chicken, turkey, pig, beef, and eggs on a ketogenic diet. Rather than processed meats like bacon and sausage, choose fresh meats, fish, and poultry, more frequently.

Dairy products and their substitutes. The ketogenic diet permits using cheese, sour cream, butter, coconut milk, cream, and unsweetened almond milk. Some provide a calcium-rich source.

Seasonings & Spices. Most spices and herbs are acceptable on a ketogenic diet if used sparingly.

Oils and Fats. Used liberally in a ketogenic diet. Include heart-healthy choices like flaxseed, avocado, olive, and walnut oils.

Fruit. Lemon flavor and a tiny dish of either blueberries or raspberries are permitted. Since they are considered fruits, tomatoes and avocados are acceptable on the keto diet. Most other fruits have too many carbohydrates to be included.

Seeds and Nuts. It is allowed in moderation and is a source of beneficial minerals and healthy lipids.

Beverages. Coffee, sparkling water, broth, tea, and water.

- **Improve your dietary intake**

Pick your oils and fats. Sausage and cream aren't the only acceptable foods on a ketogenic diet. Even though a ketogenic diet is heavy in fat, ensure you eat enough healthy fats like avocados, olive oil, avocado oil, seeds and nuts.

Make a fiber strategy. Due to the severe restrictions on fiber-containing carbohydrates, a keto diet often has minimal fiber intake. Include as many veggies as possible while staying within your net carbohydrate allotment. Chia seeds and flax seeds are other good sources of low-carb fiber. When necessary, think about taking a fiber supplement.

Increase your hydration intake and salt intake as necessary. Your fluid losses may rise following a ketogenic diet, particularly in the initial two weeks. Many negative consequences of beginning a ketogenic diet might be attributed to dehydration. Keep a water bottle nearby and sip tea or other carb-free beverages to maintain fluid intake. Half the body weight in ounces and pounds is a popular target. For instance, strive for 96 ounces or 12 cups of liquid if you weigh 192 pounds. Learn more about the requirements for fluids here. Your salt requirements may rise in the initial few weeks of the keto diet.

If you want to prevent the "keto flu," characterized by symptoms like headache, exhaustion, and dizziness, you may need to temporarily boost your salt consumption. You can immediately replenish fluid and sodium with a cup of broth. Olives, pickles, and condiments like soy sauce and salad dressing are additional low-carb, high-sodium meals.

Add a mineral or multivitamin supplement to your diet. B vitamins, calcium, magnesium, and potassium are just a few vitamins and minerals that might be lacking in a ketogenic diet, even if well-planned. The shortfalls may be filled up using a mineral or multivitamin supplement. You could need more based on the calcium you get from your more. Verify the low-carbohydrate status of your supplements. For instance, certain calcium chews and gummy pills might use your allotted amount of carbohydrates.

- **Obtain Help**

Your support network might greatly influence your ability to succeed. Inform your loved ones of your objectives and how they may help you.

Chapter 2: Go shopping - KETO GROCERY LIST

Below is a complete shopping list.

Foods to Buy

Vegetables	Meats	Seeds & Nuts
• Asparagus	• Ground Beef	• Almonds
• Brussels Sprouts	• Chicken (all cuts)	• Macadamias
• Cauliflower	• Pork	• Sunflower Seeds
• Cucumber	• Duck	• Flaxseeds
• Green Beans	• Sausages	• Pecans
• Lettuce	• Pastrami	• Walnuts
• Okra	• Smoked Deli Meats	• Peanuts (your choice)
• Peppers	• Fish & Shellfish	• Chia Seeds
• Radishes	• Bacon	• Pumpkin Seeds
• Spinach	• Beef	
• Zucchini	• Turkey	
• Artichokes	• Wild Game	
• Broccoli	• Beef Jerky	
• Cabbage	• Ham	
• Celery	• Pepperoni	
• Garlic	• Hotdogs	
• Kale		
• Mushrooms		
• Onion		

• Pumpkin • Sauerkraut • Tomatoes		
Dairy	**Fruits**	**Fats**
• Heavy Cream • Soft Cheeses • Cottage Cheese • Mayo • Butter • Hard Cheeses • Sour Cream • Greek Yogurt (low-carb)	• Berries • Lime • Avocados • Lemon • Coconut (unsweetened)	• Coconut Oil • MCT Oil • Lard • Cocoa Butter • Avocado Oil • Olive Oil • Ghee • Bacon Fat

Flour & Eggs	Pantry Items	Nut Butter Unsweetened
• Almond • Coconut • Psyllium Husk • Eggs	• Chicken Broth • Bone Broth • Pork Rinds • Beef Broth • Xanthan Gum • Tabasco • Coconut or Braggs Amino • Herbs & Spices • Salad Dressings (low-carb) • Baking Cocoa Powder • Sweeteners • Parchment Paper • Pickles	• Macadamia Nut Butter • Peanut Butter (any of your choice) • Almond Butter • Coconut Butter

Foods to Avoid

Grains	Legumes	Fruit
• Oatmeal • Flour & corn tortillas • Rye • Oats • Buckwheat • Quinoa • Barley • Pumpernickel • White • Wheat • Sourdough • Corn • Sandwich wraps • Sorghum • Rice	• Chickpeas • Pinto beans • Black-eyed peas • Green peas • Cannellini beans • Navy beans • Baked beans • Lima beans • Black beans • Lentils • Kidney beans • Great Northern beans	• Oranges • Bananas • Pears • Fruit Juices • Nectarines • Dried fruits such as dates, raisins, and dried mango • All fruit juices (excluding lime juice and lemon) • Tangerines • Pineapples • Apples • Grapes • Mangos • Peaches • Fruit smoothies
Dairy	**Vegetables**	**Protein**
• Condensed milk • Low-fat or fat-free yogurt	• Sweet potatoes • Yams • Corn	• Breaded meats • Bacon with added sugar

• Most kinds of milk • Creamed cottage cheese	• Parsnips • Potatoes • Baked potatoes • Peas • Artichoke • Cassava (Yuca)	• Other processed meats that might have hidden carbs

Beverages	Oils and other unhealthy fats

• Hot Chocolate
 	
• Grape Soda
 	
• Tonic Water (Not sugar-free)
 	
• Sports Drinks
 	
• Fruit juices
 	
• Sweetened iced tea
 	
• Mocha
 	
• Cocktails like screwdrivers, margaritas, and piña coladas
 	
• Colas   • Ginger Ale
 	
              • Root Beer
 	
• Energy Drinks (Not sugar-free)
 	
• Vitamin Water   • Lemonade
 	
              • Frappuccino
 	
• Non-light beers
	Any keto diet, including the Atkins one, must have enough fat in the eating plan. While these oils may not include carbohydrates, 2 to 4 teaspoons of additional fats per day are advised.

Chapter 3: Appetizers, Snacks & Side Dishes Recipes

Below are the recipes.

1. Rosemary Toasted Nuts

(Preparation Time: 5 minutes | Cooking Time: 10 minutes | Serving 5 | Difficulty: Easy)

Ingredients:

- 2 teaspoons fresh rosemary leaves, finely chopped
- 1 teaspoon erythritol
- ⅛ teaspoon black pepper, ground
- 200 g or 1¼ cups raw almonds
- 2 tablespoons coconut oil or ghee
- 1¼ teaspoons sea salt, finely ground
- ½ teaspoon cumin, ground
- Pinch of cayenne pepper

Instructions:

1. In a big frying pan at low heat, melt the oil. When melted, stir in the cayenne, cumin, salt, erythritol, and rosemary. Add the almonds after stirring.

2. Cook the almonds, stirring them every 30 seconds, for 5 to 8 minutes or until they become light brown. Take the food off the heat and let it cool fully before eating.

Nutritional Info: Calories: 300 kcal, Protein: 8.5g, Carb: 9g, Fat: 25.6g.

2. Mushroom Breaded Nuggets

(Preparation Time: 15 minutes | Cooking Time: 50 minutes | Serving 4 | Difficulty: Easy)

Ingredients:

- 2 eggs, large
- 1 teaspoon garlic powder
- ½ teaspoon sea salt, finely ground

- 120 ml or ½ cup honey mustard dressing, to serve (optional)

- 455 g or 1 lb. about 24 cremini mushrooms

- 55 g or ½ cup blanched almond flour

- 1 teaspoon paprika

- 2 tablespoons avocado oil

- Toothpicks (optional)

Instructions:

1. Set the oven's temperature to 350°F (177°C). Line a baking sheet with a rim using a silicone baking mat or parchment paper.

2. To make the mushroom stems level with the caps, break them off or trim them short.

3. Whisk the eggs after cracking them into a small bowl.

4. Mix the salt, paprika, garlic powder, and almond flour in a medium bowl by whisking the ingredients together.

5. One mushroom at a time, dip into the eggs, then drop into your flour mixture with the same hand, being cautious not to get flour on that hand. With a fork, turn the mushroom inside the flour mixture to cover all surfaces before transferring it to the prepared baking sheet. Repeat the process with the leftover mushrooms.

6. Oil should be drizzled over the covered mushrooms. The tops should turn brown in about 50 minutes in the oven.

7. Remove from the oven and, if desired, serve with the dressing. Provide toothpicks if serving to guests and relatives.

Nutritional Info: Calories: 332 kcal, Protein: 8g, Carb: 9.3g, Fat: 29.3g.

3. Vanilla muffins

(Preparation Time: 5 minutes | Cooking Time: 2 minutes | Serving 4 | Difficulty: Easy)

Ingredients:

- 1 beaten egg

- 1 cup water for cooking

- 1 tsp. vanilla extract

- 1 tbsp. Truvia

- 4 tbsp. coconut flour

- 1 tsp. coconut shred

- ¼ tsp. baking powder

Instructions:

1. To make a thick batter, combine all your ingredients and whisk thoroughly.

2. Inside the Ninja Foodi basket, add water. Fill the muffin tins with the batter, and then place the muffins on your Ninja Foodi rack.

3. Set Pressure mode and lower the pressure cooker's cover. High stress

4. For two minutes, bake the muffins. Utilize the rapid pressure release technique. Serve the muffins cold.

Nutritional Info: Calories: 61 kcal, Protein: 2.5g, Carb: 7g, Fat: 2.9g.

4. Liver Bites

(Preparation Time: 10 minutes + 24 hours (soaking time) | Cooking Time: 28 minutes | Serving 24 | Difficulty: Hard)

Ingredients:

- 1 tablespoon apple cider vinegar

- 455 g or 1 pound beef, ground

- 12 cloves garlic, minced

- 1 teaspoon black pepper, ground

- ½ teaspoon sea salt, finely ground

- 225 g or 8 ounces of chicken livers

- 4½ oz. or 4 strips of bacon

- 75 g or 1 cup pork rinds, crushed

- 1 tablespoon + 1 teaspoon onion powder

- 1 teaspoon thyme leaves, dried

Instructions:

1. Put the chicken livers inside a medium dish and add water to cover them. Vinegar is added. For 1 to 2 days, cover and store in the refrigerator. After rinsing, drain the livers.

2. Set the oven's temperature to 375°F (190°C). Line a baking sheet with a rim using a silicone baking mat or parchment paper.

3. Put the bacon and livers in a powerful blender, and mix until completely smooth. If a conventional food processor or blender is used, chop the bacon beforehand.

4. Place the other ingredients in a medium bowl after transferring the liver mixture. Use your hands to thoroughly combine the mixture.

5. A spoonful of the mixture should be pinched, rolled inside your hands, and placed on the baking sheet with parchment paper. Repeating the process, make another 24 balls out of the leftover liver mixture.

6. Bake all liver balls for about 25 to 28 minutes until they are 165°F (74°C) inside.

Nutritional Info: Calories: 116 kcal, Protein: 11.4g, Carb: 1.1g, Fat: 7.4g.

5. Jicama Crunchy Fries

(Preparation Time: 5 minutes | Cooking Time: 40 minutes | Serving 4 | Difficulty: Easy)

Ingredients:

- 2 tablespoons avocado oil

- 1 pinch of sea salt, finely ground

- 1 lb. or 1 medium jicama, peeled and chopped into fry-like pieces

- ½ teaspoon paprika

- 1 teaspoon fresh parsley, finely chopped

Optional (for serving):

- Sugar-free ketchup

- 105 g or ½ cup mayonnaise

Instructions:

- Set the oven's temperature to 400°F (205°C). Line a baking sheet with a rim using a silicone baking mat or parchment paper.

- Jicama pieces should be placed on a baking pan and mixed with paprika and oil. Fries should be baked for 40 minutes, turning them over halfway through.

- After taking the fries out of the oven, season them with parsley and salt, then serve. If preferred, provide the mayonnaise over the side for dipping.

Nutritional Info: Calories: 96 kcal, Protein: 1.2g, Carb: 14.7g, Fat: 3.7g.

---

6. Almond bites

(Preparation Time: 10 minutes | Cooking Time: 14 minutes | Serving 5 | Difficulty: Easy)

Ingredients:

- ¼ cup almond milk

- 2 tbsp. Butter

- ½ tsp. baking powder

- ½ tsp. vanilla extract

- 1 cup almond flour

- 1 egg, whisked

- 1 tbsp. coconut flakes

- ½ tsp. apple cider vinegar

Instructions:

- The beaten egg, apple cider vinegar, almond milk, baking powder, butter, and vanilla extract, should all be combined.

- Add coconut flakes and almond flour after stirring the mixture. Work the dough.

- Almond flour should be added extra once the dough is sticky. Make the medium-sized dough balls, and then arrange them on the rack.

- With the palm, softly press them. Cook them all for about 12 minutes at 360 degrees Fahrenheit with the cover of the air fryer.

- Verify the bite's readiness and cook for 2 minutes for a crispy crust.

Nutritional Info: Calories: 118 kcal, Protein: 2.7g, Carb: 2.4g, Fat: 11.5g.

7. Tuna Cucumber Boats

(Preparation Time: 5 minutes | Cooking Time: 0 minutes | Serving 1 | Difficulty: Easy)

Ingredients:

- 5-oz/142-g 1 can flake tuna packed inside water, drained

- 3 tablespoons mayonnaise

- 2 teaspoons fresh parsley, finely chopped

- 1 minced clove garlic

- 12 inches/ 30.5 cm long 1 English cucumber

- 1 finely diced dill pickle

- 2 tablespoons red onions, finely diced

- 1 teaspoon lemon juice

- ½ teaspoon Dijon mustard

Instructions:

1. Scoop off the seeds after cutting the cucumber in half lengthwise, and then cut each piece in half across. Place aside.

2. In a medium-sized bowl, combine the other ingredients and stir until well combined.

3. Put a lot of your tuna mixture into all hollowed-out cucumber pieces. Place on a dish, and then eat!

Nutritional Info: Calories: 527 kcal, Protein: 41.7g, Carb: 12.7g, Fat: 34.4g.

8. Tapenade

(Preparation Time: 5 minutes | Cooking Time: 0 minutes | Serving 6 | Difficulty: Easy)

Ingredients:

- 115 g or 1 cup pitted green olives

- 6 basil leaves, fresh

- 1 tablespoon parsley leaves, fresh

- Leaves from 1 sprig of fresh oregano

- 1 anchovy fillet

- 6 medium celery stalks, cut into sticks to serve

- 115 g or 1 cup pitted black olives

- 28 g or ¼ cup tomatoes in oil, sun-dried and drained

- 1 tablespoon capers

- 2 teaspoons thyme leaves, fresh

- 1 clove garlic

- 60 ml or ¼ cup olive oil

Instructions:

1. Combine all the ingredients in a blender or food processor except the celery sticks and olive oil. Until roughly chopped, pulse.

2. Add the olive oil and then pulse a few more times to blend.

3. Serve with celery sticks in a 16-ounce (475 ml) serving dish or bigger.

Nutritional Info: Calories: 167 kcal, Protein: 0.9g, Carb: 4.1g, Fat: 16.4g.

9. Vanilla Yogurt

(Preparation Time: 20 minutes | Cooking Time: 3 hours | Serving 4 | Difficulty: Easy)

Ingredients:

- ¼ cup yogurt started
- ½ tablespoon pure vanilla extract
- ½ cup milk, full-fat
- 1 cup heavy cream
- 2 teaspoons stevia

Instructions:

1. In the Ninja Foodi pot, combine the milk with the heavy cream, vanilla essence, and Stevia.
2. Sit the yogurt down and secure the cover. 3 hours of cooking in the slow cooker
3. Mix 1 cup milk and the yogurt starter in a small basin, then pour the mixture into the cooker.
4. Lock the lid and cover the Foodi with two little T-clothes.
5. 9 hours should pass to enable the yogurt to ferment. Serve after refrigeration. Enjoy!

Nutritional Info: Calories: 292 kcal, Protein: 5g, Carb: 8g, Fat: 26g.

10. Sautéed Asparagus along Tahini-Lemon Sauce

(Preparation Time: 5 minutes | Cooking Time: 10 minutes | Serving 4 | Difficulty: Easy)

Ingredients:

- 2 tablespoons avocado oil
- 16 asparagus spears, snapped off woody ends

Tahini-Lemon Sauce:

- 1 tablespoon avocado oil
- 1 clove garlic, small minced

- 1 pinch of black pepper, ground

- 2 tablespoons tahini

- 2½ teaspoons lemon juice

- 1/16 teaspoon sea salt, finely ground

- 1 to 1½ tablespoons water

Instructions:

1. Over medium heat, add the oil to a big frying pan with the asparagus. Cook for approximately 10 minutes, occasionally tossing all spears inside the oil until they become light brown.

2. Make the sauce in the interim: In a medium bowl, combine the oil, tahini, lemon juice, salt, garlic, pepper, and 1 tablespoon of water. Blend until combined. Add the extra 1/2 tbsp of water, and then whisk the dressing once more if it is too thick.

3. Arrange the cooked asparagus and top with the lemon-tahini sauce on a serving platter.

Nutritional Info: Calories: 106 kcal, Protein: 3.5g, Carb: 5.7g, Fat: 7.7g.

11.   Avocado bacon-wrapped fries

(Preparation Time: 10 minutes | Cooking Time: 18 minutes | Serving 4 | Difficulty: Easy)

Ingredients:

- 2 medium Hass avocados, pitted and peeled (around 8 oz./220 g of flesh)

- 1 lb./455 g 16 strips bacon, cut in half lengthwise

Instructions:

1. For a total of 16 fries, cut every avocado into 8 pieces in the form of fries.

2. Each avocado fry is encased in two bacon half-strips. Once finished, put it inside a big frying pan.

3. Put a splash guard on the pan and place it over medium heat. Fry for 18 minutes, 6 minutes on each side and 6 minutes on the bottom, or once crispy.

4. Take the food out of the heat right away and enjoy!

Nutritional Info: Calories: 525 kcal, Protein: 43.2g, Carb: 6.4g, Fat: 58.3g.

12.   MAC Fatties

(Preparation Time: 10 minutes | Cooking Time: 0 minutes | Serving 20 | Difficulty: Hard)

Ingredients:

- 70 g or ⅓ cup coconut oil

- 280 g or 1¾ cups macadamia nuts, salted and roasted

Spicy Cumin Flavor:

- ¼ teaspoon cayenne pepper

- ½ teaspoon cumin, ground

Garlic Herb Flavor:

- ½ teaspoon paprika

- 1¼ teaspoons oregano leaves, dried

- ½ teaspoon garlic powder

Rosemary Lemon Flavor:

- ¼ teaspoon lemon juice

- 1 teaspoon fresh rosemary, finely chopped

Turmeric Flavor:

- ¼ teaspoon ginger powder

- ½ teaspoon turmeric powder

Instructions:

1. Blend or process the oil and macadamia nuts in a food processor. Blend the mixture until it is smooth or as smooth as your blender will allow.

2. ¼ cup (87 g) of the mixture should go in each of the 4 tiny bowls.

3. Add the lemon juice and rosemary to the first bowl and mix to incorporate.

4. Cumin and cayenne pepper should be added to a second bowl and mixed.

5. Add the ginger and turmeric to the third bowl and mix to incorporate.

6. Add the paprika, oregano, and garlic powder to the fourth bowl and whisk to incorporate.

7. On the counter, place a metal mini muffin or 24-well silicone tray. If using a metal pan, insert little foil liners into 20 wells. (Avoid using paper; it will absorb all the fat.) Use roughly a spoonful of the combinations of each well when you spoon them into the wells.

8. Place in the freezer and let stand for an hour or until frozen. Directly from the freezer, enjoy.

Nutritional Info: Calories: 139 kcal, Protein: 1.1g, Carb: 1.9g, Fat: 14.1g.

13. Keto Diet Snack Plate

(Preparation Time: 10 minutes | Cooking Time: 10 minutes | Serving 1 | Difficulty: Easy)

Ingredients:

- 6 jalapeño-stuffed olives

- 1 medium Hass avocado, pitted, peeled, and sliced (around 4 oz./110 g of flesh)

- 1 tablespoon mayonnaise

- 85 g or 3 ounces salami, sliced

- 28 g or ¼ cup sauerkraut

- 1 large egg, hard-boiled, cut in half, and peeled

- 0.35-oz/10-g 1 package seaweed sheets, roasted

Instructions:

Put everything on a dish, and then start eating!

Nutritional Info: Calories: 519 kcal, Protein: 19.7g, Carb: 14.9g, Fat: 57.7g.

14. Dried tomatoes

(Preparation Time: 5 minutes | Cooking Time: 8 hours | Serving 8 | Difficulty: Easy)

Ingredients:

- 1 tablespoon basil

- 1 tablespoon onion powder

- 1 teaspoon paprika

- 5 tomatoes, medium

- 1 teaspoon cilantro

- 5 tablespoons olive oil, organic

Instructions:

1. Sliced tomatoes have been washed.

2. Combine basil, paprika, and cilantro. Stir well.

3. Add the spice combination to the pressure cooker along with the tomato slices.

4. Place a lid on after adding organic olive oil.

5. The meal should be prepared slowly for 8 hours.

6. The tomatoes must be semi-dry after the cooking process is finished. They must be taken out of the pressure cooker.

7. Warm dried tomatoes should be served.

Nutritional Info: Calories: 92 kcal, Protein: 1g, Carb: 3.8g, Fat: 8.6g.

15. Crunchy chicken skin

(Preparation Time: 10 minutes | Cooking Time: 10 minutes | Serving 7 | Difficulty: Easy)

Ingredients:

- 1 teaspoon black pepper, ground

- 9 ounces of chicken skin

- 1 teaspoon of essential olive oil, organic

- 1 teaspoon of red chili flakes

- 1 teaspoon of salt

- 2 tablespoons of butter

- 1 teaspoon of paprika

Instructions:

1. Combine paprika, chili flakes, and black pepper. Stir.

2. Chicken skin is added to the mixture and given five minutes to rest.

3. Put butter in the pressure cooker's sauté setting.

4. The chicken skin should be added as soon as the butter melts, and it should be sautéed for 10 minutes with constant tossing. Take the chicken skin out of the pressure cooker when it becomes crispy and set it on the paper towel to absorb extra oil.

5. Serve hot.

Nutritional Info: Calories: 134 kcal, Protein: 7g, Carb: 0.9g, Fat: 11.5g.

16. Ginger Cookies

(Preparation Time: 10 minutes | Cooking Time: 14 minutes | Serving 2 | Difficulty: Easy)

Ingredients:

- 1 egg
- 3 tbsp. heavy cream
- 1 tsp. Ginger, ground
- ½ tsp. baking powder
- 1 cup almond flour
- 3 tbsp. Erythritol
- 3 tbsp. Butter
- ½ tsp. cinnamon, ground

Instructions:

1. Gently whisk the egg into the bowl while beating it. Mix in the baking powder, ground cinnamon, erythritol, ginger, and heavy cream.

2. Gently stir in the butter. The non-sticky dough must be worked. Create cookies using a rolling pin, roll out the dough, and a cookie cutter.

3. Put a single layer of cookies inside the basket and secure the cover. Bake the cookies for about 14 minutes at 350 degrees Fahrenheit.

4. Once the cookies are prepared, thoroughly cool them before serving!

Nutritional Info: Calories: 172 kcal, Protein: 4.4g, Carb: 4.1g, Fat: 15.6g.

17. Radish chips and pesto

(Preparation Time: 10 minutes | Cooking Time: 0 minutes | Serving 2 | Difficulty: Easy)

Ingredients:

Pesto:

- 60 g or ⅓ heaping cup raw almonds, soaked in water for 12 hours, rinsed and drained
- 1 small clove of garlic
- 1 tablespoon apple cider vinegar
- ⅛ teaspoon sea salt, finely ground
- 60 g or 1 cup basil leaves, fresh
- 25 g or ⅓ cup fresh parsley stems and leaves
- 2 tablespoons olive oil
- 1½ teaspoons lemon juice
- 3¼ oz./90 g 20 medium radishes, thinly sliced, to serve

Instructions:

1. Put all the pesto ingredients inside a food processor or strong blender. Blend until smooth on high.

2. To a serving dish, transfer the pesto. Serve the radishes once they have been cut into slices.

Nutritional Info: Calories: 337 kcal, Protein: 8.1g, Carb: 10.2g, Fat: 29.4g.

18. Dairy-Free Queso

(Preparation Time: 10 minutes + 12 hours soaking | Cooking Time: 10 minutes | Serving 5 | Difficulty: Hard)

Ingredients:

- 120 ml or ½ cup nondairy milk

- ½ teaspoon sea salt, finely ground

- 1 yellow onion, medium sliced

- 1 tablespoon chili powder

- ¾ teaspoon garlic powder

- ½ teaspoon oregano leaves, dried

- ⅛ teaspoon cayenne pepper

- 130 g or 1 cup raw cashews

- 17 g or ¼ cup nutritional yeast

- 60 ml or ¼ cup avocado oil

- 2 cloves garlic, roughly chopped

- 1 teaspoon cumin, ground

- ¼ teaspoon onion powder

- ⅛ teaspoon paprika

- 100 g or 3½ ounces pork rinds, and 2 medium zucchinis, chopped into sticks, to serve (optional)

Instructions:

1. Put the cashews in a 12-ounce (350 ml) or big sealable container. Submerge in water. For a 12-hour soak, seal and put the container in the refrigerator. Drain and rinse the cashews after 12 hours, then combine them with the nutritional yeast, milk, and salt in a food processor or blender. Place aside.

2. Heat the oil over medium-low heat in a deep frying pan until it shimmers. Toss the onion with the ingredients after adding the garlic, onion, and spices. For approximately 10 minutes, or until the onion softens, stir your mixture every few minutes. Add the onion mixture to the blender or food processor. Blend under cover until smooth.

3. If preferred, serve the queso with pig rinds or zucchini sticks.

Nutritional Info: Calories: 300 kcal, Protein: 6.5g, Carb: 11.3g, Fat: 24g.

Chapter 4: Vegan, Vegetable & Meatless Recipes

Below are the recipes.

1. Roasted Marinated mushrooms

(Preparation Time: 10 minutes | Cooking Time: 13 minutes | Serving 6 | Difficulty: Easy)

Ingredients:

- 1 onion
- 1-ounce bay leaf
- 3 tablespoons apple cider vinegar
- 1 teaspoon of sea salt
- 10 ounces mushrooms
- 1 garlic clove
- ¼ teaspoon black-eyed peas
- 1 tablespoon olive oil
- 1 teaspoon black pepper, ground

Instructions:

1. Peel the garlic and onion cloves. Black-eyed peas are sliced and added to the veggies. Apple cider vinegar and bay leaf should be added.

2. The mushrooms should be chopped and added to the onion mixture. Black pepper and sea salt should be added.

3. Mix thoroughly, and then set aside for 10 minutes to rest. Set the sauté setting on the pressure cooker. Add all the mushroom mixture to the pressure cooker after adding the olive oil.

4. Sauté the food for 13 minutes with your pressure cooker lid closed.

5. Open your pressure cooker cover after the cooking period, and then mix well.

6. Place the mushrooms in dishes for serving.

Nutritional Info: Calories: 189 kcal, Protein: 5g, Carb: 42.6g, Fat: 3.2g.

2. Ginger broccoli soup

(Preparation Time: 5 minutes | Cooking Time: 25 minutes | Serving 4 | Difficulty: Easy)

Ingredients:

- 1 white onion, small sliced

- 420 g or 5 cups broccoli florets

- 355 ml or 1½ cups chicken bone broth

- 1½ teaspoons turmeric powder

- 55 g or ⅓ cup collagen peptides (optional)

- 3 tablespoons avocado or coconut oil

- 2 minced garlic cloves

- 400 ml 1 tin coconut milk, full-fat

- 2 inch 1 piece fresh ginger root, minced and peeled

- ¾ teaspoon sea salt, finely ground

- 40 g or ¼ cup sesame seeds

Instructions:

- In a big frying pan at medium heat, melt the oil. For approximately 10 minutes, add the garlic and onion and simmer until transparent.

- Broccoli, broth, coconut milk, ginger, salt, and turmeric, should all be added. The broccoli should be soft after 15 minutes of cooking with the cover on.

- Add all broccoli mixture to a food processor or blender. Blend in the collagen, if used, until well combined.

- Divide into 4 bowls, sprinkle 1 tablespoon of the sesame seeds on top of each dish, and enjoy!

Nutritional Info: Calories: 344 kcal, Protein: 13.3g, Carb: 12.4g, Fat: 26.8g.

3. Sriracha carrots

(Preparation Time: 10 minutes | Cooking Time: 17 minutes | Serving 7 | Difficulty: Easy)

Ingredients:

- 1 cup of water

- 2 tablespoons olive oil

- 1 pound carrots

- 2 tablespoons sriracha

- 1 teaspoon Erythritol

- ½ cup dill

- 1 teaspoon oregano

Instructions:

- The carrots should be washed, peeled, and sliced. Set the sauté setting on the pressure cooker. The pressure cooker should be filled with olive oil before adding the carrot slices.

- Add some dill and oregano to the veggies. Stirring often throughout the 15 minutes of sautéing the food.

- Add water, erythritol, and sriracha to the carrot. Mix thoroughly.

- Cook the food on Pressure mode for about 2 minutes with the pressure cooker lid closed.

- Release any leftover pressure to open the pressure cooker lid when the cooking time is complete. Onto a serving platter, place the carrots.

Nutritional Info: Calories: 74 kcal, Protein: 1.2g, Carb: 9.3g, Fat: 4.2g.

4. Roasted veggie mix

(Preparation Time: 10 minutes | Cooking Time: 30 minutes | Serving 10 | Difficulty: Easy)

Ingredients:

- 2 yellow bell peppers

- 8 ounces tomatoes

- 1 zucchini

- 2 carrots

- 4 cups beef broth

- 2 eggplants

- 1 tablespoon salt

- 2 turnips

- 1 tablespoon oregano

- 3 tablespoons sesame oil

Instructions:

1. Chop the eggplants after peeling them. Salt the eggplants, then thoroughly stir. Bell peppers with seeds removed should be chopped.

2. Chop the turnips and slice the tomatoes. Slice the zucchini.

3. Grate the carrots after peeling them. All the veggies should be added to your pressure cooker. Add the beef broth, sesame oil, and oregano.

4. Stir well, and then secure the pressure cooker cover. For thirty minutes, steam the meal.

5. Transfer the meal to serving dishes after the cooking period is over.

Nutritional Info: Calories: 107 kcal, Protein: 4g, Carb: 13.2g, Fat: 5g.

5. Cauliflower puree with scallions

(Preparation Time: 15 minutes | Cooking Time: 7 minutes | Serving 6 | Difficulty: Easy)

Ingredients:

- 4 cups of water
- 4 tablespoons butter
- 1 teaspoon chicken stock
- 1 egg yolk
- 1 head cauliflower
- 1 tablespoon salt
- 3 ounces scallions
- ¼ teaspoon sesame seeds

Instructions:

1. Cauliflower should be washed and roughly chopped. In the pressure cooker, put the cauliflower.

2. Salt and water are added. Vegetables should be cooked in pressure mode for about 5 minutes with the lid closed.

3. Open your pressure cooker cover to let the pressure out. Cauliflower should be removed from the pressure cooker and given time to rest.

4. Blend the cauliflower in a food processor. Chicken stock, butter, and sesame seeds should be added. The substance has been well blended.

5. Slice the scallions. Blend the mixture in the blender for 30 seconds after adding the egg yolk. The scallions should be added to the cauliflower puree after removing it from the blender.

6. Mix thoroughly, then plate.

Nutritional Info: Calories: 94 kcal, Protein: 2g, Carb: 3.4g, Fat: 8.7g.

6. Spinach Quiche

(Preparation Time: 10 minutes | Cooking Time: 33 minutes | Serving 4 | Difficulty: Easy)

Ingredients:

- 1 pack of spinach, frozen and thawed

- Salt and pepper to taste

- 1 tablespoon melted butter

- 5 beaten eggs, organic

- 3 cups shredded Monterey Jack Cheese

Instructions:

1. Set the Ninja Foodi to Sauté mode and wait for it to warm up before adding butter and allowing it to melt.

2. Add the spinach and cook it for 3 minutes before transferring it to a bowl.

3. In a bowl, combine eggs, cheese, salt, and pepper.

4. Place the mixture into quiche molds that have been oiled, then place the form in your Foodi.

5. Close the cover, choose "Bake/Roast," and cook for about 30 minutes at 360 degrees Fahrenheit.

6. Open the cover when finished, and then remove the dish. Serve after cutting into wedges. Enjoy!

Nutritional Info: Calories: 349 kcal, Protein: 23g, Carb: 3.2g, Fat: 27g.

7. Brussels sprouts

(Preparation Time: 7 minutes | Cooking Time: 4 minutes | Serving 6 | Difficulty: Easy)

Ingredients:

- 1 teaspoon salt

- ½ teaspoon coriander

- 1 cup chicken stock

- 1 tablespoon butter

- 13 ounces Brussels sprouts

- 1 teaspoon cumin

- ½ teaspoon chili powder

- 1 teaspoon thyme

- 1 teaspoon olive oil

Instructions:

- After cleaning, add the Brussels sprouts to the pressure cooker.

- Salt, coriander, cumin, thyme, and chili powder combine and well mixed. After thoroughly stirring, sprinkle the spice mixture over the Brussels sprouts.

- Add chicken stock, butter, and olive oil. Select Pressure mode on the pressure cooker. Snap the pressure cooker's lid shut. For 4 minutes, cook at.

- Release all pressure and open your pressure cooker cover when cooking is complete.

- Put the prepared food in dishes for serving.

Nutritional Info: Calories: 67 kcal, Protein: 3g, Carb: 7.2g, Fat: 3.5g.

8. Kale salad with spicy lime-tahini dressing

(Preparation Time: 15 minutes | Cooking Time: 0 minutes | Serving 4 | Difficulty: Easy)

Ingredients:

Salad:

- 12 radishes, thinly sliced

- 1 medium Hass avocado, pitted, peeled, and cubed

- 360 g or 6 cups de-stemmed kale leaves, roughly chopped

- 1 sliced green bell pepper

- 30 g or ¼ cup hulled pumpkin seeds

Dressing:

- 60 ml or ¼ cup lime juice

- 2 minced cloves garlic

- Handful of freshly chopped cilantro leaves

- ½ teaspoon sea salt, finely ground

- 120 ml or ½ cup avocado oil

- 60 ml or ¼ cup tahini

- 1 jalapeño pepper, finely diced and seeded

- ½ teaspoon cumin, ground

- ¼ teaspoon red pepper flakes

Instructions:

- Mix all ingredients inside a medium bowl using a whisk to prepare the dressing. Place aside.

- Assemble the salad: To soften and make the kale simpler to digest, rinse it in hot water for approximately 30 seconds. Place the kale in a big salad dish after thoroughly drying it. Toss in the leftover salad ingredients after adding them.

- Four bowls should get an equal amount of salad. Pour 14 cups (60 ml) of your dressing into each bowl before serving.

- RETAIN IT: For up to five days, store the salad and dressing in different airtight containers inside the refrigerator. The avocado should not be added to your recipe until just before serving.

Nutritional Info: Calories: 517 kcal, Protein: 10.7g, Carb: 21g, Fat: 47g.

9. Vegetable tart

(Preparation Time: 15 minutes | Cooking Time: 25 minutes | Serving 9 | Difficulty: Moderate)

Ingredients:

- 1 egg yolk

- 5 ounces tomatoes

- 1 eggplant

- 1 teaspoon salt

- 1 teaspoon black pepper, ground

- 7 ounces of goat cheese

- 7 ounces puff pastry

- 2 red bell peppers

- 1 red onion

- 3 ounces zucchini

- 1 teaspoon olive oil

- 1 tablespoon turmeric

- ¼ cup cream

Instructions:

1. Black pepper and egg yolk are thoroughly combined after whisking.

2. A rolling pin is used to roll the puff pastry. Spray some olive oil into the pressure cooker, and then add all-puff pastry.

3. The whisked egg should be spread over the puff pastry. Cut the onions and tomatoes into dice. Slice the zucchini and eggplant.

4. After combining the veggies, season them with turmeric, salt, and cream. After thoroughly combining, add the vegetable mixture to the pressure cooker.

5. Red bell peppers should be chopped and added to the pressure cooker mixture. Grate the goat cheese, and then top the tart with it.

6. Snap the pressure cooker's lid shut. Cook for 25 minutes in pressure mode. Release all pressure and open your pressure cooker cover after the food is done. Once the tart has been thoroughly cooked, take it from your pressure cooker.

7. Serve the tart by cutting it into wedges.

Nutritional Info: Calories: 279 kcal, Protein: 10g, Carb: 18.4g, Fat: 18.8g.

10.   Stewed cabbage

(Preparation Time: 10 minutes | Cooking Time: 30 minutes | Serving 7 | Difficulty: Easy)

Ingredients:

- 2 red bell pepper
- 1 cup tomato juice
- 1 teaspoon salt
- 1 teaspoon basil
- 13 ounces cabbage
- ¼ chile pepper
- 1 tablespoon olive oil
- 1 teaspoon paprika
- ½ cup chopped dill

Instructions:

1. The cabbage should be washed and cut into small pieces.

2. Use your hands to thoroughly combine the paprika, salt, and basil with the chopped cabbage.

3. Place the pressure cooker with the chopped cabbage inside. Olive oil, tomato juice, and chopped dill should all be added.

4. Red bell pepper and chile pepper should be chopped. Mix thoroughly before adding the veggies to the pressure cooker.

5. Cook the meal on "Sauté" mode for 30 minutes with your pressure cooker lid closed.

6. Once the food has finished cooking, serve it after a little rest.

Nutritional Info: Calories: 46 kcal, Protein: 1g, Carb: 6.6g, Fat: 2.2g.

11. Zucchini pizza

(Preparation Time: 10 minutes | Cooking Time: 8 minutes | Serving 2 | Difficulty: Easy)

Ingredients:

- ½ teaspoon tomato paste
- ½ teaspoon chili flakes
- 1 teaspoon olive oil
- 1 zucchini
- 5 oz. Parmesan, shredded
- ¼ teaspoon basil, dried

Instructions:

1. For boards, cut your zucchini in half. Then remove the meat from the inside and smear it with tomato paste.

2. After that, stuff zucchini with cheese shreds. Olive oil, dried basil, and chili flakes are sprinkled on them.

3. Pizzas made with zucchini should be placed inside the oven with the cover on.

4. Pizzas should be baked for 8 minutes at 375 degrees F in crisp air mode.

Nutritional Info: Calories: 331 kcal, Protein: 28.1g, Carb: 6g, Fat: 21.9g.

12.   Spicy Cauliflower Steak

(Preparation Time: 10 minutes | Cooking Time: 4 minutes | Serving 6 | Difficulty: Easy)

Ingredients:

- 2 tablespoons olive oil, extra-virgin

- 2 teaspoon ground cumin

- 1 cup fresh chopped cilantro

- 1 large head of cauliflower

- 2 teaspoons paprika

- ¾ teaspoon kosher salt

- 1 lemon, quartered

Instructions:

1. The steamer rack should be put into the Ninja Foodi. Include 1.5 cups of water.

2. Cauliflower's leaves should be removed, and the center should be trimmed to sit flat.

3. Place it carefully on your steam rack. Add salt, cumin, paprika, and olive oil to a small bowl.

4. Over the cauliflower, pour the mixture.

5. Close the cover and cook for 4 minutes at high pressure.

6. Release the pressure quickly. Slice the cauliflower into 1-inch steaks after transferring it to a cutting board.

7. Place a portion of the mixture on each dish, then top with cilantro. Dispense and savor!

Nutritional Info: Calories: 283 kcal, Protein: 10g, Carb: 18g, Fat: 19g.

Chapter 5: Pork, Beef, Lamb & Poultry Recipes

Below are the recipes.

1. Chicken and Cabbage Meatball

(Preparation Time: 7 minutes | Cooking Time: 4 minutes | Serving 4 | Difficulty: Easy)

Ingredients:

- ¼ cup heavy whip cream
- ½ teaspoon caraway seeds, ground
- ¼ teaspoon allspice, ground
- ½ cup almond milk
- 1 lb. chicken, ground
- 2 teaspoons salt
- 1½ teaspoons black pepper, ground and divided
- 4 to 6 cups chopped green cabbage
- 2 tablespoons butter, unsalted

Instructions:

1. Place the meat in a bowl.
2. Mix thoroughly after adding cream, 1 teaspoon of salt, 1/2 teaspoon of pepper, caraway, and allspice.
3. Put the mixture in the fridge for 30 minutes.
4. Scoop all mixture into the meatballs after cooling.
5. Add half the balls and half the cabbage to the Ninja Foodi pot.
6. Add the remaining balls, and then top with the rest of the cabbage.
7. Add milk, butter pats, and a sprinkling. 1 teaspoon each of salt and pepper
8. Put the cover on and cook under high pressure for 4 minutes. A rapid release of pressure.
9. Lock the lid, and then serve.

Nutritional Info: Calories: 294 kcal, Protein: 12g, Carb: 4g, Fat: 26g.

2. BBQ Chicken

(Preparation Time: 5 minutes | Cooking Time: 17 minutes | Serving 6 | Difficulty: Easy)

Ingredients:

- 1 tbsp. olive oil
- ¼ tsp. black pepper
- 1 cup hot sauce
- 2 tablespoons vinegar
- 1½ lbs. chicken thighs, skinless and boneless
- 1 tsp. paprika, ground
- 1 onion, chopped
- ¼ cup water

Instructions:

1. Add olive oil and switch the Ninja Foodi to the sauté setting. Add the chicken thighs and cook for 2 minutes on each side.

2. Sprinkle the chicken with salt and pepper, and then add the other ingredients to the saucepan.

3. Use the pressure cooker setting on the Ninja Foodi with the lid on to cook the chicken for about 15 minutes at high heat.

4. Utilize a natural steam release to relieve the pressure, and then shred the chicken with two forks. Serve both warm and cold.

Nutritional Info: Calories: 215 kcal, Protein: 17g, Carb: 1g, Fat: 16g

3. Crispy thighs and mash

(Preparation Time: 15 minutes | Cooking Time: 30 minutes | Serving 6 | Difficulty: Easy)

Ingredients:

Crispy Chicken:

- 60 ml or ¼ cup coconut oil or avocado oil, melted

- ½ teaspoon onion powder

- ¼ teaspoon black pepper, ground

- 1 lb. 3 large or 6 small skinless and boneless chicken thighs

- 1 teaspoon garlic powder

- ¼ teaspoon sea salt, finely ground

Butternut Mash:

- 2 tablespoons coconut ghee or oil

- ⅛ Teaspoon black pepper, ground

- 1½ tablespoons chicken bone broth

- 1¼ lbs. 1 medium butternut squash

- ½ teaspoon sea salt, finely ground

- 80 ml or ⅓ cup milk (regular or non-dairy)

Instructions:

1. Prepare the chicken: Set the oven's temperature to 400°F (205°C). Cut big chicken thighs in half to create 6 pieces if using them. On a baking sheet with a rim, arrange the chicken. The thighs are covered in oil; then the spices are sprinkled on top. The thighs should be turned to evenly distribute the oil and seasoning. Bake the chicken for 25 to 30 minutes or until it reaches an internal temperature of 165°F (74°C). Slice the chicken into 1.25 cm-thick (1.12 inch) pieces.

2. Make the mash in the interim: Cut the squash's meat into cubes after removing the peel and seeds. Measure out 3 cups (455 g) of your squash cubes for the mash; save the rest for another use by storing it in the refrigerator.

3. A big frying pan with medium heat is used to heat the oil. Add the salt, pepper, and squash. The squash should be gently browned after 10-15 minutes of cooking with the cover on. When the squash is soft enough to mash, add the milk and broth, cover the pan, and boil for another 15 minutes. When the squash is finished cooking, mash it in the pan using the back of a fork.

4. Divide the mash over 6 dinner plates to serve. Enjoy! Place an equal quantity of all sliced chicken thighs on each serving.

Nutritional Info: Calories: 331 kcal, Protein: 16.2g, Carb: 9.9g, Fat: 26.5g.

4. Keto-Friendly Chicken Tortillas

(Preparation Time: 7 minutes | Cooking Time: 15 minutes | Serving 4 | Difficulty: Easy)

Ingredients:

- 1 lb. boneless chicken breasts, pastured organic
- 2 tsps. Worcestershire sauce, gluten-free
- 1 tsp. Salt
- ½ tsp. paprika
- 1 tbsp. avocado oil
- ½ cup orange juice
- 1 tsp. garlic powder
- ½ tsp. chili powder

Instructions:

1. Put your Ninja Foodi in sauté mode, add some oil, and then wait for it to warm up.
2. Add the chicken, and then combine the other ingredients in a bowl.
3. Over the chicken, pour the mixture.
4. Place the cover on and cook under high pressure for 15 minutes.
5. Over ten minutes, naturally release the pressure.
6. Chicken should be shredded with green salad, lettuce or cabbage.

Nutritional Info: Calories: 338 kcal, Protein: 23g, Carb: 10g, Fat: 23g.

5. Hot Spicy Paprika Chicken

(Preparation Time: 10 minutes | Cooking Time: 24 minutes | Serving 4 | Difficulty: Easy)

Ingredients:

- Pepper and salt

- ½ cup sweet onion, chopped

- 2 teaspoons paprika, smoked

- 2 tablespoons parsley, chopped

- 4 pieces chicken breast

- 1 tbsp. olive oil

- ½ cup heavy whip cream

- ½ cup sour cream

Instructions:

1. Lightly season the chicken with pepper and salt.

2. Put your Ninja Foodi in sauté mode, add some oil, and then wait for it to warm up.

3. After adding it, it should take around 15 minutes to adequately brown the chicken on both sides.

4. Chicken should be taken out and placed on a platter.

5. Place an onion in a pan over medium heat, sauté for 4 minutes, or until soft, then stir in the cream and paprika and allow the liquid to a boil.

6. Add the chicken back to the skillet, along with any juices.

7. Place the cover on the Ninja Foodi and cook the whole mixture for 5 minutes at high pressure.

8. Over ten minutes, naturally release the pressure.

9. Sour cream has been added; serve and enjoy!

Nutritional Info: Calories: 389 kcal, Protein: 25g, Carb: 4g, Fat: 30g.

6. Cream of Mushroom–Stuffed Chicken

(Preparation Time: 10 minutes | Cooking Time: 45 minutes | Serving 4 | Difficulty: Easy)

Ingredients:

- 200 g or 7 ounces cremini mushrooms, chopped

- 3 teaspoons parsley, dried and divided

- ¼ teaspoon black pepper, ground

- 1 teaspoon onion powder

- 120 ml or ½ cup milk (regular or non-dairy)

- 3 tablespoons avocado oil, coconut oil, or ghee

- 4 cloves garlic, minced

- ¾ teaspoon sea salt, divided and finely ground

- 455 g or 1 pound skin-on chicken breasts, boneless

- 1 teaspoon garlic powder

- 280 g or 4 cups spinach to serve

Instructions:

1. Set the oven's temperature to 400°F (205°C). Line a baking sheet with a rim using a silicone baking mat or parchment paper.

2. A big frying pan with medium heat is used to heat the oil. Add 2 teaspoons of parsley, garlic, ¼ teaspoon of salt, and a pinch of pepper with the mushrooms. Ten minutes of sautéing after tossing to coat.

3. To open each chicken breast like a book, slice it horizontally, halting the knife about ½ inch (1.25 cm) via the other side. Be cautious not to cut through the chicken breasts completely. The easiest technique is with a sharp knife, holding it stable with your hand on the breast.

4. Open the chicken breasts and place them on the prepared baking sheet. Each opened breast should have a quarter of your mushroom mixture inside the center. Scatter any remaining mushroom mixture in the pan next to the chicken.

5. To enclose the filling, fold the chicken breasts over. Garlic powder, the last teaspoon of parsley, onion powder, and the last teaspoon of salt should all be sprinkled over the filled chicken breasts.

6. Directly into the pan, pour the milk in the space between the chicken breasts.

7. Bake the chicken for 30 to 35 minutes or until it reaches an internal temperature of 165°F (74°C).

8. 4 dinner plates should each get some spinach. On each dish, distribute the filled chicken breasts. Drizzle all spinach using the rich pan juices. Note: Divide the stuffed breasts into parts and serve them on equal numbers of plates. If you don't wind up with 1 breast, half every person in the packet.

Nutritional Info: Calories: 388 kcal, Protein: 38.2g, Carb: 4.3g, Fat: 24.3g.

7. Chili Rubbed Chicken

(Preparation Time: 10 minutes | Cooking Time: 30 minutes | Serving 2 | Difficulty: Easy)

Ingredients:

- 1 tbsp. chili powder
- Ground black pepper, to taste
- 1 tsp. garlic powder
- 2 chicken thighs
- 1 tablespoon Paprika
- 2 tablespoons salt
- 1 tsp. Onion powder
- 1 tsp. cumin, ground
- 1 tbsp. olive oil

Instructions:

1. Combine all the spices in a bowl, and then put it aside.

2. Olive oil should be used to coat the chicken thighs before being seasoned.

3. Turn your Ninja Foodi to 375 degrees, add the spiced chicken to the cook and crisp basket, and finish cooking.

4. Set the timer for about 30 minutes and place the basket into the Ninja Foodi.

5. Serve when still heated.

Nutritional Info: Calories: 230 kcal, Protein: 15g, Carb: 7g, Fat: 16g.

8. BBQ beef and slaw

(Preparation Time: 10 minutes | Cooking Time: 45 minutes (4 to 6 hours additional) | Serving 4 | Difficulty: Moderate)

Ingredients:

BBQ Beef:

- 240 ml or 1 cup beef bone broth

- 80 g or ½ cup barbecue sauce, sugar-free

- 455 g or 1 pound beef chuck roast, boneless

- ½ teaspoon sea salt, finely ground

Slaw:

- 120 ml or ½ cup poppy seed dressing, sugar-free

- 255 g or 9 ounces coleslaw mix

Instructions:

1. A slow or pressure cooker should include the chuck roast, stock, and salt. Secure the cover and cook for 45 minutes at high pressure if utilizing a pressure cooker. Let the lid come off naturally when everything is finished to escape the pressure. If using a slow cooker, cook on high for about 4 hours or low for about 6 hours.

2. Almost all the liquid should be drained away when the meat has finished cooking, leaving just 1/4 cup (60 ml) in the cooker. With two forks, shred the meat; add the barbecue sauce; and mix to combine.

3. In a salad dish, combine all coleslaw mix and dressing. Toss to combine.

4. Enjoy the barbecued beef and coleslaw by dividing them among four dinner plates, putting the steak on the bottom and the coleslaw on top.

Nutritional Info: Calories: 354 kcal, Protein: 23.9g, Carb: 2.9g, Fat: 26.7g.

9. Coffee Braised Pulled Beef

(Preparation Time: 15 minutes | Cooking Time: 35 minutes | Serving 6 | Difficulty: Hard)

Ingredients:

For Rub:

- 1 tablespoon cacao powder
- 1 teaspoon ginger, ground
- 1 teaspoon crushed red pepper flakes
- 2 pounds beef chuck roast grass-fed, trimmed and chopped into 1½-inch cubes
- 2 tablespoons finely ground coffee
- 1 tablespoon paprika, smoked
- 1 teaspoon red chili powder
- Salt and ground black pepper

For Sauce:

- ½ cup brewed coffee
- 2 tablespoons lemon juice, fresh
- 1 cup beef broth, homemade
- 1 yellow onion, medium chopped
- Salt and ground black pepper, as needed

Instructions:

1. Combine all the rub ingredients inside a small bowl except the roast.
2. Use a lot of the rub mixture to coat the chuck roast.
3. To make the sauce, combine all the ingredients inside a food processor and process until smooth.
4. Place the roast in the Ninja Foodi pot and evenly distribute the sauce on top.

5. Put the pressure lid on the Ninja Foodi and turn the pressure valve to the Seal position to close it.

6. Choose Pressure and set the timer for 35 minutes on High.

7. To start cooking, click Start/Stop.

8. Put the valve on Vent, then release naturally.

9. Put the roast in a basin and shred the flesh with two forks.

10. Add the pot sauce on top before serving.

Nutritional Info: Calories: 573 kcal, Protein: 41.1g, Carb: 3.7g, Fat: 42.8g.

10. Beef Jerky

(Preparation Time: 15 minutes | Cooking Time: 7 hours | Serving 6 | Difficulty: Moderate)

Ingredients:

- 2 tablespoon Worcestershire sauce

- Salt, as needed

- ¼ cup soy sauce, low-sodium

- 2 tablespoon Erythritol

- 1½ pounds beef eye of round grass-fed, cut in ¼-inch slices

Instructions:

1. Beat all the ingredients in a bowl—aside from the beef—until the sugar completely dissolves.

2. Place the beef pieces and marinate in a large plastic bag that can be sealed.

3. To coat, seal your bag and massage.

4. Overnight marinating in the refrigerator.

5. After removing the beef slices from the refrigerator, drain them and throw away the marinade.

6. Put the beef slices in a single layer in the Cook & Crisp Basket.

7. In the Ninja Foodi pot, arrange the Cook & Crisp Basket.

8. Select Dehydrate and close your Ninja Foodi with Crisping Lid.

9. Set the thermostat to 155 degrees Fahrenheit for seven hours.

10. To start cooking, click Start/Stop.

Nutritional Info: Calories: 199 kcal, Protein: 33.5g, Carb: 1.7g, Fat: 5.6g.

11. Spicy Pulled Beef

(Preparation Time: 15 minutes | Cooking Time: 1 hour 30 minutes | Serving 10 | Difficulty: Hard)

Ingredients:

- 5 peeled garlic cloves
- 2 tablespoons lime juice, fresh
- 1 tablespoon cumin, ground
- ½ teaspoon cloves, ground
- 3 pounds beef bottom round roast grass-fed, trimmed and chopped into 3-inch pieces
- 1 teaspoon olive oil
- ½ onion, medium
- 3 tablespoons chipotles inside adobo sauce
- 1 tablespoon oregano, dried and crushed
- ½ teaspoon cayenne pepper
- 1 cup water
- Salt and ground black pepper
- 3 bay leaves

Instructions:

1. Until smooth, combine onion, chipotles, garlic, lime juice, cumin, oregano, cayenne, and cloves, in a blender with the water.

2. Evenly sprinkle black pepper and salt over the meat.

3. Place all oil in the pot and choose Ninja Foodi's Sauté/Sear option.

4. To start cooking and heat for around 2-3 minutes, press Start/Stop.

5. When the meat is thoroughly browned, add it and simmer for approximately 5 minutes.

6. After stopping the cooking by pressing Start/Stop, toss in your pureed mixture and bay leaves.

7. Put the pressure lid on the Ninja Foodi and turn the pressure valve to the Seal position to close it.

8. Choose Pressure and set the timer for 65 minutes on High.

9. To start cooking, click Start/Stop.

10. Change the valve's setting to Vent and perform a quick release.

11. Transfer the meat to a bowl using a slotted spoon and shred it with two forks.

12. Stir and add 1 ½ cups of the liquid that was set aside.

13. Serve right away.

Nutritional Info: Calories: 266 kcal, Protein: 41.6g, Carb: 1.8g, Fat: 9.2g.

12. Bacon Wrapped Beef Tenderloins

(Preparation Time: 15 minutes | Cooking Time: 12 minutes | Serving 4 | Difficulty: Moderate)

Ingredients:

- 4 grass-fed beef tenderloin filets, center-cut

- Salt and ground black pepper

- 8 bacon strips

- 2 tablespoons divided olive oil

Instructions:

1. Secure each filet with toothpicks.

2. Each filet should be uniformly seasoned with black pepper and salt after being oil-coated.

3. Put the Reversible Rack into the Ninja Foodi pot.

4. Select Broil for 5 minutes while the Ninja Foodi with Crisping Lid is closed.

5. For the preheating to start, press Start/Stop.

6. Open the cover after preheating.

7. Over the Reversible Rack, arrange the beef filets.

8. With the crisping lid closed, choose Broil for about 12 minutes.

9. To start cooking, click Start/Stop.

10. Once they are halfway done, flip the filets.

11. Before serving, spread the filets on a plate for approximately 10 minutes.

12. Each beef filet should have 2 bacon strips wrapped around the outside of it.

Nutritional Info: Calories: 841 kcal, Protein: 87g, Carb: 0.8g, Fat: 52g.6 | Difficulty: Moderate)

13. Fajita Beef

(Preparation Time: 7 minutes | Cooking Time: 7 hours | Serving 4 | Difficulty: Easy)

Ingredients:

- 3 bell peppers, sliced and seeded

- 2 pounds of boneless grass-fed beef, sliced

- ½ tin diced tomatoes with green chiles, sugar-free

- 2 tablespoons butter

- 1 yellow sliced onion

- 2 tablespoons fajita seasoning

Instructions:

1. Place your butter in the saucepan and choose the Sauté/Sear mode on Ninja Foodi.

2. To start cooking and heat for around 2-3 minutes, press Start/Stop.

3. Cook the onion and bell pepper for two to three minutes after adding them.

4. After adding the fajita spice, cook the meat for 4-5 minutes.

5. To stop cooking and then stir in the tomato can, press Start/Stop.

6. Select Slow Cooker, and then close your Ninja Foodi with a crisping cover.

7. Set for seven hours on low.

8. To start cooking, click Start/Stop.

9. Serve warm.

Nutritional Info: Calories: 658 kcal, Protein: 22.5g, Carb: 6.1g, Fat: 58.9g.

14. The Premium Red Pork

(Preparation Time: 10 minutes | Cooking Time: 40 minutes | Serving 6 | Difficulty: Moderate)

Ingredients:

- 2 tablespoons maple syrup

- 1 tablespoon blackstrap molasses

- 1 teaspoon salt

- 1-piece ginger, smashed and peeled

- 2 pounds of pork belly

- 3 tablespoons sherry

- 2 tablespoons coconut amino

- 1/3 cup water

- Few sprigs of cilantro for garnishing

Instructions:

1. Put the pork chunks in a saucepan with just enough water to cover them, and then set it over medium heat. Let the water reach a boil.

2. Drain and clean the ice cubes after three minutes of boiling to eliminate contaminants.

3. Place them to one side. Sauté mode on your Ninja Foodi, then adds maple syrup.

4. Add the cooked cubes and brown them for one minute.

5. Add the ingredients to the stew after 10 minutes, and then bring the whole mixture to a boil. Cook for about 25 minutes at high pressure with the lid closed.

6. Allow all pressure to decrease naturally.

7. Open the lid and go back to Sauté mode on your Ninja Foodi.

8. Simmer the mixture once enough liquid is reduced to coat the ice cubes. Serve with cilantro as a garnish. Enjoy!

Nutritional Info: Calories: 355 kcal, Protein: 31g, Carb: 16g, Fat: 13g.

15. Crispy Pork with thyme-lemon cauliflower rice

(Preparation Time: 5 minutes | Cooking Time: 40 minutes | Serving 4 | Difficulty: Moderate)

Ingredients:

Crispy Pork:

- 38 g or ½ cup pork rinds, crushed

- 1 teaspoon oregano leaves, dried

- ½ teaspoon sea salt, finely ground

- 455 g or 1 pound pork chops, boneless

- 55 g or ¼ cup coconut ghee or oil, or 60 ml ¼ cup avocado oil

- 1 teaspoon garlic powder

- 1 teaspoon thyme leaves, dried

- ¼ teaspoon black pepper, ground

Thyme-Lemon Cauliflower Rice:

- 1 white onion, small diced

- 60 ml or ¼ cup chicken bone broth

- ½ teaspoon sea salt, finely ground

- 680 g or 1½ lbs. 1 medium head cauliflower, or 3 cups (375 g) cauliflower, pre-riced

- 4 minced cloves of garlic

- 2 tablespoons lemon juice

- 6 sprigs leaves of fresh thyme

Instructions:

1. In a big frying pan, warm the oil over medium-low heat.

2. Crushed pork rinds, oregano, garlic powder, salt, thyme, and pepper should all be combined in a medium-sized bowl while the oil is heated. One at a time, add all pork chops and coat them in the mixture after stirring to combine. Transfer the chops to your frying pan after they are well coated.

3. The pork chops should be properly seared after 10 minutes on each side.

4. Use pre-riced cauliflower and go on to Step 5 instead. Otherwise, trim the cauliflower's base off and separate the florets. The florets should be placed in a blender or food processor and pulsed three to four times to create pieces that are 1/4 inch (6 mm) in size.

5. Transfer all chops to a clean dish when the pork has cooked for 20 minutes, but keep the cooking oil in the pan. Add the broth, salted, lemon juiced and riced cauliflower. Approximately 15 minutes of cooking time should be allotted for the cauliflower rice to become soft yet not mushy while stirring occasionally.

6. Slice all pork chops into 12-inch (1.25-cm) thick pieces as you wait. Add the sliced pork into the skillet after the cauliflower rice is cooked. Cook the pork uncovered for 5 minutes if necessary to ensure complete cooking.

7. On 4 dinner plates, distribute the cauliflower rice and pork. Garnish with thyme leaves.

Nutritional Info: Calories: 419 kcal, Protein: 34g, Carb: 6g, Fat: 27.7g.

16. Butter and Dill Pork Chops

(Preparation Time: 10 minutes | Cooking Time: 20 minutes | Serving 4 | Difficulty: Easy)

Ingredients:

- 4 pieces pork loin chops, ½ inch thick

- ½ teaspoon pepper

- ½ cup white wine vinegar

- 2 tablespoons butter, unsalted

- ½ teaspoon salt

- 16 baby carrots
- ½ cup chicken broth

Instructions:

1. Set the Sauté mode on your Ninja Foodi. Sprinkle salt and pepper on the chops.

2. Chops should be thrown into a saucepan and cooked for four minutes.

3. Cook and brown the remaining chops before transferring the first batch to a dish.

4. 1 tablespoon of butter should be added. Put the dill and carrots in the cooker and heat for approximately a minute.

5. As the stock comes to a boil, pour in all wine and scrape any browned pieces off the bottom of the stove.

6. Add the broth and stir. Bring the chops back to your pot.

7. Lock the cover and cook it under high pressure for about 18 minutes.

8. Of course, let the pressure out by leaving it alone for 8 minutes.

9. Open, and then serve using some sauce on top.

Nutritional Info: Calories: 296 kcal, Protein: 17g, Carb: 2g, Fat: 25g.

17. Happy Burrito Bowl Pork

(Preparation Time: 10 minutes | Cooking Time: 5 minutes | Serving 4 | Difficulty: Easy)

Ingredients:

- 1 sliced onion
- 1 chopped garlic clove
- 1 pound pulled pork
- ½ cup chicken broth
- 6 cups chopped cabbage
- 1 and ½ tablespoons pork lard
- 2 sliced bell peppers

- Salt and pepper to taste

- ½ cup of chicken pork

- 6 cups chopped lettuce

- ¼ cup guacamole

Instructions:

1. On the Sauté setting of your Ninja Foodi, add the lard, let it melt, then add the onion and bell pepper.

2. Cook for two minutes while stirring. Salt, Garlic, and pepper are added.

3. Stir well. Add chicken pork and pulled pork.

4. Lock the cover and cook for one minute under high pressure. A rapid release of pressure

5. Put green cabbage and lettuce in serving dishes, and then top with pulled pork.

6. Serve after adding guacamole on top. Enjoy!

Nutritional Info: Calories: 417 kcal, Protein: 75g, Carb: 6g, Fat: 95g.

---

18. Pork Carnitas

(Preparation Time: 10 minutes | Cooking Time: 25 minutes | Serving 4 | Difficulty: Easy)

Ingredients:

- 1 teaspoon salt

- ½ teaspoon cumin

- 6 garlic cloves, crushed and peeled

- 2 pounds pork butt, chopped into 2-inch pieces

- ½ teaspoon oregano

- 1 yellow onion, cut into half

- ½ cup chicken broth

Instructions:

1. Put the pork in a pan in your Ninja Foodi.

2. Make sure the pork is well-seasoned by adding cumin, salt, and oregano and mixing thoroughly.

3. Add the squeezed orange to the insert pan after taking the orange and squeezing it all over it.

4. Add the onions and garlic cloves. Fill the pan with 1/2 cup of chicken broth.

5. Lock the Ninja Foodi's lid, ensuring the valve is well secured.

6. Set the pressure to high and let it 20 minutes to cook.

7. Release the pressure immediately once the timer sounds.

8. Remove the orange, the onions, and the garlic cloves by opening the lid.

9. Set the temperature on the Nina Foodi to medium-high and choose the Sauté option.

10. Simmer the liquid for ten to fifteen minutes.

11. Press the stop button once most of your liquid has been decreased.

12. Close the "Air Crisp" cover on the Ninja Foodi. Choose "Pressure Broil" and set the timer for 8 minutes.

13. Put the meat in wrappers after taking it out. Enjoy with cilantro as a garnish!

Nutritional Info: Calories: 355 kcal, Protein: 43g, Carb: 9g, Fat: 13g.

19. Ham-Stuffed Turkey Rolls

(Preparation Time: 8 minutes | Cooking Time: 20 minutes | Serving 8 | Difficulty: Easy)

Ingredients:

- 8 ham slices

- Salt and pepper

- 4 tablespoons sage leaves, fresh

- 8 turkey cutlets

- 2 tablespoons butter, melted

Instructions:

1. Salt and pepper turkey cutlets before serving.

2. Each turkey cutlet is securely wrapped in ham slices after being rolled.

3. Butter each roll and delicately arrange sage leaves on top of each cutlet.

4. Place them on your Ninja Foodi Lock lid, choose "Bake/Roast," and bake them at 360 degrees Fahrenheit for 10 minutes.

5. Lock the cover again and bake for 10 minutes after gently flipping it.

6. Serve and savor once finished!

Nutritional Info: Calories: 467 kcal, Protein: 56g, Carb: 1.7g, Fat: 24g.

20. Turkey Cutlets

(Preparation Time: 10 minutes | Cooking Time: 22 minutes | Serving 4 | Difficulty: Easy)

Ingredients:

- 1 lb. turkey cutlets
- 1 tsp. turmeric powder
- 1 tsp. Greek seasoning
- 2 teaspoons olive oil
- ½ cup almond flour

Instructions:

1. Greek seasoning, almond flour, and turmeric powder should all be combined in a bowl.

2. Turkey cutlets should be dredged in the basin and let soak for 30 minutes.

3. Set your Ninja Foodi to Sauté mode, add oil, and let it warm up.

4. Add cutlets, and then cook for two minutes.

5. Lock the cover and cook for 20 minutes at low-medium pressure.

6. Over ten minutes, naturally release the pressure.

7. Remove the dish, serve, and enjoy!

Nutritional Info: Calories: 340 kcal, Protein: 36g, Carb: 3.7g, Fat: 19g.

Chapter 6: Fish & Seafood Recipes

Below are the recipes.

1. Salmon and Kale

(Preparation Time: 5 minutes + 2 hours marinating | Cooking Time: 15 minutes | Serving 4 | Difficulty: Easy)

Ingredients:

- 180 ml or ¾ cup vinaigrette of choice

- 240 g or 4 cups de-stemmed kale leaves

- ¼ teaspoon sea salt, finely ground

- 455 g or 1 pound salmon fillets chopped into 4 equal portions

- 1 red onion, small sliced

- ¼ teaspoon red pepper flakes

Instructions:

1. Place the salmon inside a small bowl and cover with a vinaigrette. For two hours of marinating, place covered in the refrigerator.

2. Add the whole marinade and the salmon to a big frying pan when you cook. Place the fish in a circle and reduce the heat to medium- or low. Salmon should be cooked for 6 minutes on each side to achieve searing.

3. Push the salmon to the pan's edges for space for the kale after the salmon has been prepared for 12 minutes. Toss the kale inside the pan drippings after adding salt, red pepper, and flakes. The greens should wilt after 3 minutes of cooking under cover.

4. Serve the braised kale and salmon fillets on four dinner plates.

Nutritional Info: Calories: 438 kcal, Protein: 26.3g, Carb: 5.8g, Fat: 33g.

2. Scallops and Mozza Broccoli Mash

(Preparation Time: 5 minutes | Cooking Time: 35 minutes | Serving 4 | Difficulty: Easy)

Ingredients:

Mozza Broccoli Mash:

- 570 g or 6 cups broccoli florets

- 2-in/5-cm 1 piece fresh ginger root, grated

- 70 g or ½ cup mozzarella cheese (regular or dairy-free), shredded

- 55 g or ¼ cup coconut ghee or oil, or 60 ml ¼ cup avocado oil

- 4 minced cloves of garlic

- 160 ml or ⅔ cup chicken bone broth

Scallops:

- ¼ teaspoon sea salt, finely ground

- 2 tablespoons coconut oil, ghee, or avocado oil

- 455 g or 1 pound sea scallops

- ¼ teaspoon black pepper, ground

- Lemon wedges to serve

Instructions:

1. Making the mash: Warm the oil slowly in a big frying pan. Cook the broccoli, ginger, and garlic for 5 minutes, uncovered, or once the garlic is aromatic.

2. Add the liquid, cover, and simmer on low for 25 minutes when the broccoli is quickly mashed.

3. Prepare the scallops for around 5 minutes until the broccoli is done: After patting the scallops dry, sprinkle salt and pepper over both sides. A medium-sized frying pan with medium heat is used to heat the oil.

4. Add the scallops to the heated oil. Cook each side for 2 minutes or until lightly browned.

5. Add the cheese and mash using a fork after cooking the broccoli. On top of the scallops, divide the mashed potatoes among 4 dinner plates. Enjoy your meal with lemon wedges!

Nutritional Info: Calories: 353 kcal, Protein: 19.2g, Carb: 12g, Fat: 25.4g.

3. Noodles and glazed Salmon

(Preparation Time: 5 minutes | Cooking Time: 20 minutes | Serving 4 | Difficulty: Moderate)

Ingredients:

- 60 ml or ¼ cup coconut amino

- 2 tablespoons apple cider vinegar

- 4 minced cloves of garlic

- 455 g or 1 pound salmon fillets, cut into 4 equal portions

- 2 sliced green onions

- 1 teaspoon sesame seeds

- 75 ml or ¼ cup plus 2 tablespoons avocado oil, divided

- 2 tablespoons plus 2 teaspoons tomato paste

- 2-in/5-cm 1 piece fresh ginger root, grated

- ½ teaspoon sea salt, finely ground

- 7-oz/198-g 2 packages konjac noodles or the same amount of other low-carb noodles of choice

- Handful of cilantro leaves, fresh and roughly chopped

Instructions:

1. Heat 2 tablespoons of oil on medium heat in a big frying pan.

2. Make the sauce once the oil is warming up: Mix the tomato paste, ginger, vinegar, garlic, coconut amino, salt, and the remaining ¼ cup of oil in a small bowl.

3. After adding the salmon to the heated pan, lower the heat and slather it with the sauce. Any leftover sauce should be drizzled immediately into the pan. 15 minutes on low heat, covered, until seared and just barely heated through.

4. When the salmon is finished cooking, pile it up in the pan on one side, leaving room for the noodles. Toss the green onions and noodles in the remaining sauce after adding them to the pan. Then, top the noodles with the cooked salmon. Just enough time to heat your noodles is another three to five minutes of cooking.

5. Salmon should be topped with cilantro and sesame seeds. On four dinner plates, distribute the noodles and salmon, top with any remaining pan sauce, and serve.

Nutritional Info: Calories: 333 kcal, Protein: 24.7g, Carb: 8.2g, Fat: 22.4g.

4. Buttered Salmon

(Preparation Time: 10 minutes | Cooking Time: 10 minutes | Serving 2 | Difficulty: Easy)

Ingredients:

- Salt and black pepper, ground

- 2 salmon fillets

- 1 tablespoon melted butter

Instructions:

1. Place the Cook & Crisp Basket in the Ninja Foodi pot after greasing it.

2. Select Air Crisp and shut the Ninja Foodi with Crisping Lid.

3. For five minutes, set the thermostat to 360 degrees Fahrenheit.

4. To start preheating, press "Start/Stop."

5. After each salmon fillet has been seasoned with salt and pepper, drizzle it with melted butter.

6. Open the cover after preheating.

7. Put all salmon fillets in a single layer in the Cook & Crisp Basket that has been prepared.

8. Select Air Crisp and shut the Ninja Foodi having Crisping Lid.

9. For 10 minutes, raise the temperature to 360 degrees Fahrenheit.

10. To start cooking, click Start/Stop.

11. Serve warm.

Nutritional Info: Calories: 276 kcal, Protein: 33.1g, Carb: 1g, Fat: 16.3g.

5. Glazed Salmon Fillets

(Preparation Time: 10 minutes | Cooking Time: 13 minutes | Serving 2 | Difficulty: Easy)

Ingredients:

- 2 tablespoons bacon syrup

- 2 teaspoons water

- 3 tablespoons soy sauce, low-sodium

- 2 teaspoons lemon juice, fresh

- 2 salmon fillets

Instructions:

1. Mix all the ingredients in a small bowl except the salmon.

2. Reserve roughly half of your mixture in a small basin.

3. The remaining mixture is added, and the fish is well coated.

4. For approximately two hours, marinate covered in the refrigerator.

5. In the Ninja Foodi pot, arrange the Cook & Crisp Basket.

6. Select Air Crisp and shut the Ninja Foodi with Crisping Lid.

7. For five minutes, set the thermostat to 355 degrees Fahrenheit.

8. For the preheating to start, press Start/Stop.

9. Open the cover after preheating.

10. Salmon fillets should be added to the Cook & Crisp Basket.

11. Select Air Crisp and shut the Ninja Foodi with Crisping Lid.

12. For 13 minutes, set the thermostat to 355 degrees Fahrenheit.

13. To start cooking, click Start/Stop.

14. Flip all salmon fillets over and brush with the leftover marinade after 8 minutes.

15. Serve warm.

Nutritional Info: Calories: 181 kcal, Protein: 28.2g, Carb: 4g, Fat: 4.7g.

6. Seasoned Catfish

(Preparation Time: 15 minutes | Cooking Time: 23 minutes | Serving 4 | Difficulty: Easy)

Ingredients:

- 2 tablespoons Italian seasoning

- 1 tablespoon olive oil

- 4 catfish fillets

- Salt and black pepper, ground

- 1 tablespoon chopped fresh parsley

Instructions:

1. Place the Cook & Crisp Basket inside the Ninja Foodi pot after greasing it.

2. Select Air Crisp and shut the Ninja Foodi with Crisping Lid.

3. For five minutes, set the thermostat to 400 degrees Fahrenheit.

4. For the preheating to start, press Start/Stop.

5. After liberally seasoning all fish fillets with salt, pepper, and seasoning, drizzle oil over them.

6. Open the cover after preheating.

7. The Cook & Crisp Basket should be filled with the catfish fillets.

8. Select Air Crisp and shut the Ninja Foodi with Crisping Lid.

9. For 20 minutes, set the thermostat to 400 degrees Fahrenheit.

10. To start cooking, click Start/Stop.

11. When the fish fillets are halfway done, flip them.

12. Serve hot with parsley as a garnish.

Nutritional Info: Calories: 205 kcal, Protein: 17.7g, Carb: 0.8g, Fat: 14.2g.

7. Parsley Tilapia

(Preparation Time: 15 minutes | Cooking Time: 1 hour 30 minutes | Serving 6 | Difficulty: Moderate)

Ingredients:

- Salt and black pepper, ground

- 3 teaspoons lemon rind, fresh and grated finely

- 2 tablespoon butter, unsalted and melted

- 6 tilapia fillets

- ½ cup chopped yellow onion

- ¼ cup parsley, freshly chopped

Instructions:

1. Grease the Ninja Foodi pot.

2. Make liberal use of black pepper and salt while seasoning the tilapia fillets.

3. Put the tilapia fillets in the Ninja Foodi pot that has been prepared.

4. Spread the onion, parsley, and lemon rind equally over the fillets before adding the melted butter.

5. Select Slow Cooker, and then close your Ninja Foodi with a crisping cover.

6. Set for 1 ½ hours on Low.

7. To start cooking, click Start/Stop.

8. Serve warm.

Nutritional Info: Calories: 133 kcal, Protein: 21.3g, Carb: 1.3g, Fat: 4.9g.

8. Cod with Tomatoes

(Preparation Time: 15 minutes | Cooking Time: 6 minutes | Serving 4 | Difficulty: Easy)

Ingredients:

- 2 tablespoons rosemary, freshly chopped

- 2 minced garlic cloves

- Salt and black pepper, ground

- 1-pound halved cherry tomatoes

- 4 cod fillets

- 1 tablespoon olive oil

Instructions:

1. Half of the cherry tomatoes and the rosemary should be placed in the base of a big heatproof bowl that has been oiled.

2. Place the remaining tomatoes on top, and then cover them with the fish fillets.

3. Garlic should be sprinkled on top of the oil.

4. Place the bowl in the Ninja Foodie's bottom.

5. Put the pressure lid on the Ninja Foodi and turn its pressure valve to the Seal position to close it.

6. Choose Pressure and set the timer for 6 minutes on High.

7. To start cooking, click Start/Stop.

8. Change the valve's setting to Vent and perform a quick release.

9. Place the tomatoes and fish fillets on plates for serving.

10. Serve after seasoning with black pepper and salt.

Nutritional Info: Calories: 149 kcal, Protein: 21.4g, Carb: 6g, Fat: 5g.

9. Parmesan Tilapia

(Preparation Time: 15 minutes | Cooking Time: 4 hours | Serving 4 | Difficulty: Moderate)

Ingredients:

- ¼ cup mayonnaise

- Salt and black pepper, ground

- 2 tablespoons cilantro, freshly chopped

- ½ cup grated Parmesan cheese

- ¼ cup lemon juice, fresh

- 4 tilapia fillets

Instructions:

1. All ingredients—except the tilapia fillets and cilantro—should be combined in a bowl.

2. Evenly spread the mayonnaise mixture over the fillets.

3. Over a big piece of foil, arrange the filets.

4. To seal the fillets, wrap all foil around them.

5. Place the foil package in the Ninja Foodi's bottom.

6. Select Slow Cooker, and then close your Ninja Foodi with a crisping cover.

7. Set for 3 to 4 hours on low.

8. Press "Start/Stop" to start the stove.

9. Serve hot with cilantro as a garnish.

Nutritional Info: Calories: 223 kcal, Protein: 25.2g, Carb: 0.3g, Fat: 13.5g.

10. Crispy Tilapia

(Preparation Time: 15 minutes | Cooking Time: 14 minutes | Serving 4 | Difficulty: Easy)

Ingredients:

- 1 packet dry dressing mix, ranch-style

- 2 eggs, organic

- ¾ cup crushed pork rinds

- 2½ tablespoons olive oil

- 4 tilapia fillets

Instructions:

1. Place the Cook & Crisp Basket inside the Ninja Foodi pot after greasing it.

2. Select Air Crisp and shut the Ninja Foodi with Crisping Lid. For five minutes, set the thermostat to 355 degrees Fahrenheit. To start preheating, press "Start/Stop."

3. The eggs should be beaten in a small basin. Add the oil, ranch dressing, and pork rinds to another bowl and stir once a crumbly mixture forms.

4. Fish fillets are dipped in egg, and then coated with a combination of pig rinds.

5. Open the cover after preheating. Put all tilapia fillets in a single layer in the Cook & Crisp Basket that has been prepared.

6. Select Air Crisp and shut the Ninja Foodi with Crisping Lid.

7. For 14 minutes, preheat the oven to 350 degrees Fahrenheit. To start cooking, click Start/Stop. Serve warm.

Nutritional Info: Calories: 304 kcal, Protein: 38g, Carb: 0.4g, Fat: 16.8g.

Chapter 7: Sauces & Dressing Recipes

Below are the recipes.

1. Easy & quick barbecue sauce

(Preparation Time: 5 minutes | Cooking Time: 0 minutes | Serving 1 ¼ cups | Difficulty: Easy)

Ingredients:

- 80 ml or ⅓ cup (80 ml) water
- 2 tablespoons coconut amino
- ½ teaspoon garlic powder
- ½ teaspoon paprika
- ¼ teaspoon black pepper, ground
- 80 ml or ⅓ cup balsamic vinegar
- 6-oz/170-g 1 tin tomato paste
- 1 tablespoon Dijon mustard
- ½ teaspoon onion powder
- ½ teaspoon sea salt, finely ground

Instructions:

1. In a 16-ounce (475 ml) or big airtight container, combine all the ingredients.
2. Shake the cover while incorporating.

Nutritional Info: Calories: 11 kcal, Protein: 0.4g, Carb: 2.1g, Fat: 0.1g.

2. Teriyaki sauce and marinade

(Preparation Time: 5 minutes | Cooking Time: 0 minutes | Serving 1 ½ cups | Difficulty: Easy)

Ingredients:

- 60 ml or ¼ cup coconut amino
- 1 tablespoon apple cider vinegar

- 1 teaspoon ginger powder

- 240 ml or 1 cup of light-tasting oil, such as light olive oil or avocado oil

- 2 tablespoons erythritol, confectioners'-style

- 1 teaspoon garlic powder

- 1 teaspoon sea salt, finely ground

Instructions:

1. In a 16-ounce (475 ml) or big airtight container, combine all the ingredients. Shake the cover while incorporating.

2. Shake the container slightly before serving and take a bite.

Nutritional Info: Calories: 85 kcal, Protein: 0g, Carb: 0.7g, Fat: 9.1g.

3. Avocado mousse

(Preparation Time: 2 minutes | Cooking Time: 10 minutes | Serving 7 | Difficulty: Easy)

Ingredients:

- 3 tbsp. Erythritol

- 1 tsp. butter

- 1 tsp. of cocoa powder

- 2 avocados, cored and peeled

- 1/3 cup heavy cream

- 1 tsp. vanilla extract

Instructions:

1. For five minutes, preheat the Ninja Foodi in the sauté mode. Meanwhile, puree the avocado and combine it with the erythritol.

2. Melt the butter after adding it to the saucepan. Stir thoroughly after adding the mashed avocado combination. Cocoa powder should be added and mixed well. Three minutes to sauté the ingredients. While doing this, whisk your heavy cream for two minutes at high speed. Put the heated avocado mash in a bowl and cool with cold water.

3. Add the vanilla extract and heavy cream after the avocado mash has warmed to room temperature. Gently stir to create swirls of white chocolate.

4. Place the mousse in tiny cups and refrigerate for 4 hours.

Nutritional Info: Calories: 144 kcal, Protein: 1.3g, Carb: 10.5g, Fat: 13.9g.

4. Ranch dressing

(Preparation Time: 5 minutes | Cooking Time: 0 minutes | Serving 2 cups | Difficulty: Easy)

Ingredients:

- 120 ml or ½ cup full-fat coconut milk

- 2 tablespoons fresh chives, sliced

- 1 tablespoon white onions, minced

- 1 tablespoon apple cider vinegar

- ¼ teaspoon sea salt, finely ground

- 210 g or 1 cup mayonnaise

- 3 tablespoons fresh parsley, finely chopped

- 2 small minced cloves of garlic

- 1 tablespoon fresh dill, finely chopped

- 1 tablespoon lemon juice

- ⅛ teaspoon black pepper, ground

Instructions:

In a 20-ounce (600 ml) or big airtight container, combine all the ingredients. Shake the cover while incorporating. Shake the container slightly before serving and take a bite.

Nutritional Info: Calories: 57 kcal, Protein: 0.1g, Carb: 0.4g, Fat: 6.1g.

5. Thai dressing

(Preparation Time: 5 minutes | Cooking Time: 0 minutes | Serving 1 cup | Difficulty: Easy)

Ingredients:

- 60 ml or ¼ cup full-fat coconut milk

- 2 tablespoons coconut amino

- 1 tablespoon lime juice

- ½ teaspoon cayenne pepper

- 70 g or ¼ cup smooth almond butter, unsweetened

- 2 tablespoons apple cider vinegar

- 2 tablespoons sesame oil, toasted

- 1 teaspoon garlic powder

- ½ teaspoon sea salt, finely ground

Instructions:

1. In a 12-ounce (350 ml) or big airtight container, combine all the ingredients. Shake the cover while incorporating. Shake the container slightly before serving and take a bite.

2. Keep for up to 5 days in the refrigerator.

Nutritional Info: Calories: 22 kcal, Protein: 0.1g, Carb: 0.7g, Fat: 2g.

Chapter 8: Dessert Recipes

Below are the recipes.

1. Raspberry dump cake

(Preparation Time: 10 minutes | Cooking Time: 30 minutes | Serving 10 | Difficulty: Easy)

Ingredients:

- 1 ½ cup coconut flour
- ¼ cup Erythritol
- 1 tbsp. melted butter
- ½ tsp. vanilla extract
- ½ cup raspberries
- 1/3 cup almond milk
- 1 whisked egg
- 1 tsp. baking powder
- 1 tsp. lemon juice

Instructions:

1. Mix the dry ingredients well. Add the egg, butter, and almond milk, after that.
2. Lemon juice and vanilla extract are added. Stir your mixture well. Get a liquid batter right away.
3. Put the raspberries in a layer into the silicone mold. Over the raspberries, pour the batter.
4. Put the mold on your rack and put the Ninja Foodi basket over it.
5. Put the air fryer's cover on and choose Bake. The cake should be baked for about 30 minutes at 350°F.
6. After baking, thoroughly refrigerate the cake. Flip over and place on the serving platter.

Nutritional Info: Calories: 107 kcal, Protein: 4.3g, Carb: 15.1g, Fat: 4.5g.

2. Brownie batter

(Preparation Time: 5 minutes | Cooking Time: 4 minutes | Serving 5 | Difficulty: Easy)

Ingredients:

- ¼ cup heavy cream
- 1 tbsp. Erythritol
- 3 tbsp. butter
- 1 oz. dark chocolate
- 1/3 cup almond flour
- 3 tbsp. cocoa powder
- ½ tsp. vanilla extract

Instructions:

1. To create the layer, spread the almond flour in the springform pan. Put the springform pan into the pot afterward, and close the air fryer cover.

2. The almond flour should be cooked for 3 minutes at 400 degrees F or until brown.

3. Meanwhile, add heavy cream and cocoa powder; whisk all heavy cream until smooth.

4. Add erythritol and vanilla essence. Ninja Foodi's almond flour should be taken out and well chilled.

5. Put the dark chocolate and butter in the saucepan and set the temperature to Sauté for 1 minute.

6. Add the softened butter to your heavy cream mixture. Then include almond flour and chocolate. Serve the mixture after homogenizing it.

Nutritional Info: Calories: 159 kcal, Protein: 2.5g, Carb: 9g, Fat: 14.9g.

3. Ketone Gummies

(Preparation Time: 40 minutes | Cooking Time: 5 minutes | Serving 8 | Difficulty: Easy)

Ingredients:

- 8 hulled strawberries (frozen and defrosted or fresh)

- 2 teaspoons exogenous ketones

- 120 ml or ½ cup lemon juice

- 2 tablespoons gelatin, unflavored

- Silicone mold having eight 2-tablespoon or bigger cavities

Instructions:

1. Have your preferred silicone mold on hand. To produce 8 gummies, people prefer to utilize a big silicone ice cube tray and scoop 2 teaspoons of the ingredients into each cavity. If you don't have a silicone mold, use a metal or silicone baking pan that is 8 inches (20 cm) square. If you use a metal pan, line it using parchment paper and drape some over the edges for simple removal.

2. In a food processor or blender, combine the strawberries, gelatin, and lemon juice; process until smooth. After transferring the mixture into the small saucepan, boil it for 5 minutes at a low temperature or until it is extremely liquid.

3. Exogenous ketones are added after the heat is turned off.

4. Pour the mixture into your baking pan or divide it among the mold's eight chambers. Place in the refrigerator and let stand for 30 minutes. Cut into 8 squares if utilizing a baking pan.

Nutritional Info: Calories: 19 kcal, Protein: 3.2g, Carb: 1.2g, Fat: 0.2g.

4. Soft-Serve Chocolate Ice Cream

(Preparation Time: 55 minutes | Cooking Time: 0 minutes | Serving 4 | Difficulty: Easy)

Ingredients:

- 40 g or ¼ cup collagen peptides or protein powder (optional)

- 2 tablespoons smooth almond butter, unsweetened

- 1 tablespoon erythritol or 3 drops liquid stevia

- 13½-oz/400-ml 1 tin coconut milk, full-fat

- 25 g or ¼ cup unflavored MCT oil powder (optional)

- 2 tablespoons cocoa powder

- 1 teaspoon vanilla extract

Instructions:

1. Put all the ingredients using a food processor or blender. Blend until well combined and uniform.

2. Place the mixture in the freezer for about 30 minutes after dividing it among 4 freezer-safe serving dishes. Remove from the freezer after 30 minutes and mash using a fork once the ice cream is creamy. If it's still too fluid and doesn't become soft-serve consistency when you mash it, put it in the freezer for 15 minutes before mashing it with a fork.

3. Enjoy right now.

Nutritional Info: Calories: 419 kcal, Protein: 5.8g, Carb: 9g, Fat: 46.6g.

5. Pumpkin pie

(Preparation Time: 10 minutes | Cooking Time: 25 minutes | Serving 6 | Difficulty: Easy)

Ingredients:

- ¼ cup heavy cream
- 1 tbsp. butter

- 1 tbsp. pumpkin puree

- 1 tsp. Pumpkin spices

- 1 cup coconut flour

- 1 egg, whisked

- 2 tbsp. liquid stevia

- 1 tsp. Apple cider vinegar

- ½ tsp. baking powder

Instructions:

1. Baking powder, liquid stevia, heavy cream, melted butter, and apple cider vinegar should all be combined.

2. Add coconut flour and pumpkin puree. Spices of pumpkin are now added, and the dough is smoothed.

3. Place the Ninja Foodi basket with the batter inside, and then shut the air fryer lid.

4. The "Bake" mode to 360 degrees Fahrenheit. For 25 minutes, bake the pie. Once the allotted time has passed, allow the pie to cool until room temperature.

Nutritional Info: Calories: 127 kcal, Protein: 3.8g, Carb: 14.2g, Fat: 6.6g.

6. Superpower Fat Bombs

(Preparation Time: 45 minutes | Cooking Time: 0 minutes | Serving 8 | Difficulty: Easy)

Ingredients:

- 40 g or ¼ cup collagen peptides or protein powder

- 2 tablespoons cocoa powder

- 1 tablespoon cacao nibs

- 1 tablespoon plus 1 teaspoon confectioners'-style erythritol or 4 drops liquid stevia

- Silicone mold along 8 2-tablespoon or larger cavities (optional)

- 145 g or ⅔ cup cacao butter, coconut oil, or ghee, melted

- 25 g or ¼ cup MCT oil powder, unflavored

- 2 tablespoons flax seeds, roughly ground

- 1 teaspoon instant coffee granules

- Pinch of sea salt, finely ground

Instructions:

1. Have your preferred silicone mold on hand. We prefer to produce 8 cubes using a large silicone ice cube tray and spoon 2 teaspoons of the ingredients into each well. Turning this into a bark works great also if you don't have a silicone mold. Use an 8-inch (20-cm) square metal or silicone baking pan, lining it with parchment paper and hanging some over the edges for easy removal.

2. In a medium-sized bowl, combine all the ingredients and whisk until well combined and smooth.

3. Pour the mixture into the baking pan or divide it among the 8 holes in the silicone mold. When using cacao butter, transfer to the refrigerator and set for 15 minutes; when using coconut oil or ghee, let set for 30 minutes. For serving, divide the bark into 8 pieces using a baking sheet.

4. Store in an airtight container for up to 10 days in the refrigerator or two months in the freezer. No need to defrost; enjoy directly from the freezer.

Nutritional Info: Calories: 136 kcal, Protein: 5.8g, Carb: 3g, Fat: 12.3g.

7. Blueberry crumbles with cream topping

(Preparation Time: 5 minutes | Cooking Time: 25 minutes | Serving 6 | Difficulty: Easy)

Ingredients:

- 110 g or 1 cup blanched almond flour

- 65 g or ⅓ cup erythritol

- 1 teaspoon cinnamon, ground

- 510 g or 18 ounces of blueberries, frozen or fresh

- 70 g or ⅓ cup coconut oil or ghee at room temperature

- 2 tablespoons coconut flour

- 250 g or 1 cup coconut cream, or 240 ml or 1 cup full-fat coconut milk to serve

Instructions:

1. Set the oven's temperature to 350°F (177°C).

2. Inside an 8-inch (20-cm) square baking sheet, add the blueberries.

3. Mix the almond flour, erythritol, oil, coconut flour, and cinnamon; stir with a fork until crumbly. Crumble over the blueberries' tops.

4. When the top is brown, bake for another 22 to 25 minutes.

5. After taking it out of the oven, let it rest for ten minutes before dividing it into six serving dishes. Add 2 to 3 tablespoons of the coconut cream to the top of each bowl.

Nutritional Info: Calories: 388 kcal, Protein: 4.9g, Carb: 12.7g, Fat: 33.4g.

60-Day Meal Plan

Days	Breakfast	Snack	Lunch	Snack	Dinner
Day 1	Vanilla muffins	Almond Bites	BBQ Chicken	Roasted Marinated mushrooms	Crispy Tilapia
Day 2	Superpower Fat Bombs	Tuna Cucumber Boats	Sriracha carrots	Ginger Cookies	Beef Jerky
Day 3	Mushroom Breaded Nuggets	Vanilla Yogurt	Salmon and Kale	Avocado mousse	Keto-Friendly Chicken Tortillas
Day 4	Vegetable tart	Avocado bacon-wrapped fries	Crispy thighs and mash	Ketone Gummies	Parmesan Tilapia
Day 5	Pumpkin pie	Ginger broccoli soup	Turkey Cutlets	Brownie batter	Bacon Wrapped Beef

					Tenderloins
Day 6	Liver Bites	Raspberry dump cake	The Premium Red Pork	Stewed cabbage	Cod with Tomatoes
Day 7	Blueberry crumbles with cream topping	Rosemary Toasted Nuts	Scallops and Mozza Broccoli Mash	Roasted veggie mix	Hot Spicy Paprika Chicken
Day 8	Spinach Quiche	Brussels sprouts	Chili Rubbed Chicken	Keto Diet Snack Plate	Crispy Pork with thyme-lemon cauliflower rice
Day 9	Tapenade	Kale salad with spicy lime-tahini dressing	Happy Burrito Bowl Pork	Soft-Serve Chocolate Ice Cream	Cream of Mushroom–Stuffed Chicken
Day 10	Zucchini Pizza	Jicama Crunchy Fries	Seasoned Catfish	Radish chips and pesto	BBQ beef and slaw
Day 11	Vanilla muffins	Almond Bites	BBQ Chicken	Roasted Marinated mushrooms	Crispy Tilapia
Day 12	Superpower Fat Bombs	Tuna Cucumber Boats	Sriracha carrots	Ginger Cookies	Beef Jerky
Day 13	Mushroom Breaded Nuggets	Vanilla Yogurt	Salmon and Kale	Avocado mousse	Keto-Friendly Chicken Tortillas

Day 14	Vegetable tart	Avocado bacon-wrapped fries	Crispy thighs and mash	Ketone Gummies	Parmesan Tilapia
Day 15	Pumpkin pie	Ginger broccoli soup	Turkey Cutlets	Brownie batter	Bacon Wrapped Beef Tenderloins
Day 16	Liver Bites	Raspberry dump cake	The Premium Red Pork	Stewed cabbage	Cod with Tomatoes
Day 17	Blueberry crumbles with cream topping	Rosemary Toasted Nuts	Scallops and Mozza Broccoli Mash	Roasted veggie mix	Hot Spicy Paprika Chicken
Day 18	Spinach Quiche	Brussels sprouts	Chili Rubbed Chicken	Keto Diet Snack Plate	Crispy Pork with thyme-lemon cauliflower rice
Day 19	Tapenade	Kale salad with spicy lime-tahini dressing	Happy Burrito Bowl Pork	Soft-Serve Chocolate Ice Cream	Cream of Mushroom– Stuffed Chicken
Day 20	Zucchini Pizza	Jicama Crunchy Fries	Seasoned Catfish	Radish chips and pesto	BBQ beef and slaw
Day 21	Vanilla muffins	Almond Bites	BBQ Chicken	Roasted Marinated mushrooms	Crispy Tilapia

Day 22	Superpower Fat Bombs	Tuna Cucumber Boats	Sriracha carrots	Ginger Cookies	Beef Jerky
Day 23	Mushroom Breaded Nuggets	Vanilla Yogurt	Salmon and Kale	Avocado mousse	Keto-Friendly Chicken Tortillas
Day 24	Vegetable tart	Avocado bacon-wrapped fries	Crispy thighs and mash	Ketone Gummies	Parmesan Tilapia
Day 25	Pumpkin pie	Ginger broccoli soup	Turkey Cutlets	Brownie batter	Bacon Wrapped Beef Tenderloins
Day 26	Liver Bites	Raspberry dump cake	The Premium Red Pork	Stewed cabbage	Cod with Tomatoes
Day 27	Blueberry crumbles with cream topping	Rosemary Toasted Nuts	Scallops and Mozza Broccoli Mash	Roasted veggie mix	Hot Spicy Paprika Chicken
Day 28	Spinach Quiche	Brussels sprouts	Chili Rubbed Chicken	Keto Diet Snack Plate	Crispy Pork with thyme-lemon cauliflower rice

Day 29	Tapenade	Kale salad with spicy lime-tahini dressing	Happy Burrito Bowl Pork	Soft-Serve Chocolate Ice Cream	Cream of Mushroom–Stuffed Chicken
Day 30	Zucchini Pizza	Jicama Crunchy Fries	Seasoned Catfish	Radish chips and pesto	BBQ beef and slaw
Day 31	Vanilla muffins	Almond Bites	BBQ Chicken	Roasted Marinated mushrooms	Crispy Tilapia
Day 32	Superpower Fat Bombs	Tuna Cucumber Boats	Sriracha carrots	Ginger Cookies	Beef Jerky
Day 33	Mushroom Breaded Nuggets	Vanilla Yogurt	Salmon and Kale	Avocado mousse	Keto-Friendly Chicken Tortillas
Day 34	Vegetable tart	Avocado bacon-wrapped fries	Crispy thighs and mash	Ketone Gummies	Parmesan Tilapia
Day 35	Pumpkin pie	Ginger broccoli soup	Turkey Cutlets	Brownie batter	Bacon Wrapped Beef Tenderloins
Day 36	Liver Bites	Raspberry dump cake	The Premium Red Pork	Stewed cabbage	Cod with Tomatoes
Day 37	Blueberry crumbles with cream	Rosemary Toasted Nuts	Scallops and Mozza Broccoli	Roasted veggie mix	Hot Spicy Paprika Chicken

			Mash		
Day 38	Spinach Quiche	Brussels sprouts	Chili Rubbed Chicken	Keto Diet Snack Plate	Crispy Pork with thyme-lemon cauliflower rice
Day 39	Tapenade	Kale salad with spicy lime-tahini dressing	Happy Burrito Bowl Pork	Soft-Serve Chocolate Ice Cream	Cream of Mushroom–Stuffed Chicken
Day 40	Zucchini Pizza	Jicama Crunchy Fries	Seasoned Catfish	Radish chips and pesto	BBQ beef and slaw
Day 41	Vanilla muffins	Almond Bites	BBQ Chicken	Roasted Marinated mushrooms	Crispy Tilapia
Day 42	Superpower Fat Bombs	Tuna Cucumber Boats	Sriracha carrots	Ginger Cookies	Beef Jerky
Day 43	Mushroom Breaded Nuggets	Vanilla Yogurt	Salmon and Kale	Avocado mousse	Keto-Friendly Chicken Tortillas
Day 44	Vegetable tart	Avocado bacon-wrapped fries	Crispy thighs and mash	Ketone Gummies	Parmesan Tilapia
Day 45	Pumpkin pie	Ginger broccoli soup	Turkey Cutlets	Brownie batter	Bacon Wrapped Beef

					Tenderloins
Day 46	Liver Bites	Raspberry dump cake	The Premium Red Pork	Stewed cabbage	Cod with Tomatoes
Day 47	Blueberry crumbles with cream topping	Rosemary Toasted Nuts	Scallops and Mozza Broccoli Mash	Roasted veggie mix	Hot Spicy Paprika Chicken
Day 48	Spinach Quiche	Brussels sprouts	Chili Rubbed Chicken	Keto Diet Snack Plate	Crispy Pork with thyme-lemon cauliflower rice
Day 49	Tapenade	Kale salad with spicy lime-tahini dressing	Happy Burrito Bowl Pork	Soft-Serve Chocolate Ice Cream	Cream of Mushroom– Stuffed Chicken
Day 50	Zucchini Pizza	Jicama Crunchy Fries	Seasoned Catfish	Radish chips and pesto	BBQ beef and slaw
Day 51	Vanilla muffins	Almond Bites	BBQ Chicken	Roasted Marinated mushrooms	Crispy Tilapia
Day 52	Superpower Fat Bombs	Tuna Cucumber Boats	Sriracha carrots	Ginger Cookies	Beef Jerky
Day 53	Mushroom Breaded Nuggets	Vanilla Yogurt	Salmon and Kale	Avocado mousse	Keto-Friendly Chicken Tortillas

Day 54	Vegetable tart	Avocado bacon-wrapped fries	Crispy thighs and mash	Ketone Gummies	Parmesan Tilapia
Day 55	Pumpkin pie	Ginger broccoli soup	Turkey Cutlets	Brownie batter	Bacon Wrapped Beef Tenderloins
Day 56	Liver Bites	Raspberry dump cake	The Premium Red Pork	Stewed cabbage	Cod with Tomatoes
Day 57	Blueberry crumbles with cream topping	Rosemary Toasted Nuts	Scallops and Mozza Broccoli Mash	Roasted veggie mix	Hot Spicy Paprika Chicken
Day 58	Spinach Quiche	Brussels sprouts	Chili Rubbed Chicken	Keto Diet Snack Plate	Crispy Pork with thyme-lemon cauliflower rice
Day 59	Tapenade	Kale salad with spicy lime-tahini dressing	Happy Burrito Bowl Pork	Soft-Serve Chocolate Ice Cream	Cream of Mushroom–Stuffed Chicken
Day 60	Zucchini Pizza	Jicama Crunchy Fries	Seasoned Catfish	Radish chips and pesto	BBQ beef and slaw

Conclusion

The ketogenic diet promotes the body to get into ketosis, when it burns fat for energy instead of carbs. It is a high-fat and low-carb diet. It may cause weight reduction, better blood sugar regulation, more satiety, and lower cholesterol. However, it may be difficult to maintain and has potential drawbacks, including a higher risk of vitamin shortages and a detrimental effect on athletic performance. Before beginning any new diet, it is crucial to speak with a medical practitioner and to be aware of any dietary allergies or intolerances. Although the ketogenic diet is an effective means of shedding pounds and improving some health indicators, it is not for everyone.

A healthcare expert should be consulted, nutritional shortages should be considered, meals should be planned, macronutrients should be monitored, social circumstances should be anticipated, and assistance should be requested to guarantee the diet is reliable and acceptable. When choosing a diet, it's crucial to consider sustainability and environmental effect. Before beginning, the ketogenic diet should be addressed with a healthcare provider since it may not be suited for everyone. It may not be suitable for those with certain medical problems or medicines, may be restrictive, and may have drawbacks, including a higher risk of vitamin deficiencies. Before beginning any new diet, getting a physician's or nutritionist's advice is essential.

We provided a complete grocery list and quick recipes in this book to prepare you for the keto diet. You may consume a huge range of meals while following the keto diet. Appetizers, snacks, side dishes, vegetables, meat, poultry, fish, sauces, and desserts. While easily losing weight, you may enjoy the tastiest meals.

KETO DIET FOR WOMEN OVER 60

Chapter 1: What Happens To Women's Bodies After 60

Your body changes as you age, which is not always bad; it's simply different. Understanding what to expect can help you welcome these changes and alert you to what you can do to speed up the process. While some of these changes may be gradual and subtle, others may appear to occur suddenly. No matter when they occur, it's critical to understand that they're normal.

Ways Your Body Changes As You Age
Cardiovascular System: Your heart and blood arteries grow more inflexible as you age, and the heart fills with blood less quickly. The more inflexible the arteries are, the less room they have to expand as blood is pushed through them, which is why older persons are more likely to develop high blood pressure. A healthy older heart still functions normally, but it simply cannot pump as much blood or at the same rate as a younger heart. Because of this, older athletes often don't perform as well as younger ones. The death rate from heart-related disorders has decreased due to the numerous medical advancements accomplished during the past 20 years.
As you age, your heart and arteries get more rigid; therefore, it's critical to take all reasonable steps to maintain the health of your cardiovascular system. A nutritious diet and physical activity, particularly aerobic exercise, are two excellent ways to accomplish this.

Lungs: As you become older, your rib cage's muscles and diaphragm weaken. Additionally, the lungs lose some of their elasticity, reducing the amount of oxygen that is inhaled. This can make breathing challenging for smokers or anyone with a lung disease. Your lungs lose their ability to fend off illnesses as they deteriorate. These bacteria might linger and cause issues because they cannot spread germs without a good stiff cough.
The two best activities you can engage in to enhance lung health are:
- Avoid smoking
- Regularly engage in aerobic activity of some kind.

Exercise will provide your lungs the greatest opportunity to continue supplying your body with oxygen allowing you to stay active because your lungs aren't what they once were.

Immune System: As you age, your immune system becomes less effective. According to MedilinePlus, this may result in the following issues:

- Your immune system tends to react to stimuli more slowly, raising your risk of getting sick.
- Vaccines like those for the flu and pneumonia could not be as effective or durable as they once were.
- Because you have fewer immune cells as you age, your body recovers itself more slowly.
- You have a higher chance of getting cancer because as you become older, your body becomes less capable of identifying and repairing cell flaws.

An autoimmune illness is one where your immune system unintentionally targets and kills healthy bodily tissue. It's essential to take good care of yourself to help you keep your immune system as strong as possible. Get the vaccines your doctor advises, such as those for pneumonia, shingles, pneumococcal disease, and the flu (you can receive a high-dose flu vaccine starting at age 65). You can maintain a balanced diet, exercise, quit smoking, and consume less alcohol while building a robust immune system.

Urinary Tract: The urinary tract system often continues to function normally, barring any diseases or illnesses that affect it. If you're over 60, you've undoubtedly realized that you have to get up at least once throughout the night to use the bathroom. This is typical for this age group because as you get older, your bladder's capacity declines. Additionally, when the bladder muscles deteriorate, it may become harder to empty your bladder and shut the urinary sphincter, which might lead to leakage. These problems may lead to urinary incontinence.

Bones and Joints: Your bones and joints start to age beyond the age of 60. You absorb less calcium from your diet as you become older. Without calcium, your bones deteriorate and become brittle and feeble. Your body's ability to metabolize calcium is aided by vitamin D, which declines with age. Osteopenia (moderate loss of bone density) or osteoporosis may arise from a drop in calcium and vitamin D levels (severe loss of bone density). When osteoporosis appears, your chance of fracture and break increases significantly. Osteoporosis may be avoided by maintaining a healthy weight and engaging in weight-bearing exercises to promote bone density. You might want to discuss calcium and vitamin D supplements with your doctor.

Physical Changes As You Age

After many years of usage, your joints' surrounding cartilage may thin out, making movement painful. This cartilage deteriorates with time, making mobility difficult and perhaps dangerous. Osteoarthritis, a fairly common aging condition, may eventually develop from this. Unfortunately, wear and tear from years of usage causes joint discomfort, and surgery is now the only option to reverse it. Your doctor might occasionally recommend vitamins to aid with the discomfort. You might want to bring up this during your next appointment.

Muscle Tone and Body Fat: Around 30, your body begins to develop fat and lose muscle tone. The loss of muscle mass can be pretty substantial by the time you reach 60. According to MedilinePlus, only approximately 10 to 15% of muscle mass is lost as people age.

The rest is a result of inactivity and a poor diet. The good news is that you can maintain or improve your muscle tone even after you become 60.

Ways Your Body Changes After You Turn 60

Strength training, often known as resistance training, is essential to maintaining and regaining muscular tone via regular exercise. Eating healthily goes hand in hand with regular exercise. Together, these two substances can reduce body fat and improve muscular tone. With aging, body fat tends to rise. In this period of life, it's simple to develop a sedentary lifestyle as a habit. It's simple to develop the daily habit of doing virtually nothing, especially nothing physical because you become tired more quickly than you used to. Your chance of having diseases like diabetes is elevated by increased body fat. You can maintain a healthy body fat percentage by exercising regularly and eating a balanced diet.

Eyesight: You'll likely notice a difference in your vision by age 60. You could notice changes in your sense of color, a loss of close vision, and an increasing need for stronger lighting to read and discern details. These are generally caused by the lenses in your eyes stiffening and turning yellow. Your eyes may experience various physical changes as you age:

- Your eyes' whites can start to turn yellow.
- The whites of your eyes may develop a few specks of color.
- A gray-white ring may appear around the surface of the eye.
- Muscle loss may cause your lower lid to start drooping. If you lose fat around your eyes, it might make your eyes look sunken.

You'll probably notice as you get older that your eyes are often dry. To solve this issue, lubricating eye drops can be used. These changes to your eyes and vision are consequences of aging. See an eye doctor if they are painful or if you detect a significant change.

Hearing: Some hearing loss is not genuinely age-related; rather, it results from environmental exposure over time. Age-related hearing impairments, though, exist, such as the inability to perceive high-pitched noises. With aging, one's ability to detect high-pitched noises significantly decreases. Presbycusis is the name given to this age-related hearing loss. The ability to grasp what others are saying is the biggest problem with presbycusis. Consonants are difficult to hear because they are often uttered in a higher tone than vowels, caused by a mix of high-pitched voices, mainly those of women and children. Unfortunately, it ultimately gets harder to detect lower-pitched tones as well. Hearing difficulties might also result from earwax buildup and background noise. You can improve your hearing by maintaining clean ears and wearing hearing aids.

Teeth: As you reach 60, cavities become a major problem, mostly because of dry mouth. Dry mouth is not a problem exclusive to old age, but it is a side effect of many medications older people take for other illnesses. Gum disease is another problem that frequently arises especially as you age. While it is painless, if addressed, it can result in several issues, including tooth loss. After 60, mouth cancer becomes a risk as well.

Oral cancer typically has no discomfort in its early stages, and early identification can save lives. After age 60, your body will undergo physical changes. Your mouth, gums, and teeth can all benefit greatly from routine dental checkups. Early diagnosis saves money while also saving lives.

Skin: Your skin changes as you get older. It gets drier, thinner, less elastic, and more wrinkled. Many things in the skin start to decrease, such as elastin, collagen, the layer of fat under the skin, nerve endings, sweat glands, blood vessels, and pigment-producing cells. The lack of these things causes your skin to become easily bruised and torn, sag and bag, crack and peel, and get age spots and wrinkles. A reduced sensitivity to discomfort also raises your risk of experiencing a heat stroke.

Body Changes After 50 and 60

You may be at risk for vitamin D insufficiency once you become 60 because your skin can no longer produce vitamin D from exposure to sunshine. If you want to prevent this problem, discuss taking a supplement with your doctor. Even while it's best to take care of your skin when you're young, there are still things you can do to protect it in the future. You can start using moisturizers and sunscreen, undergo surgical procedures like laser treatments, and your doctor may prescribe some prescription drugs.

Accepting Physical Changes After 60

Aging is a privilege. Many people have remarked that they would have taken better care of their bodies if they had known they would live thus long. That sentence undoubtedly has a lot of truth for several people. While there is nothing you can do to change what you did or didn't do in the past, you can go forward and take the best possible care of yourself right now.

Practically all aspects of your evolving physique may be improved with regular exercise and a healthy diet. So stay active, eat healthily, and enjoy the rest of your life.

Chapter 2: Why is Weight Loss After 60 Hard?

Let's face it; it isn't easy to lose weight after 60. We lose the ability to consume anything we want as our bodies age. Suddenly, tracking calories and steps is necessary to beat weight. To understand why maintaining a healthy weight has suddenly become so challenging, read on for a list of 9 practical strategies to lose weight, remain in shape, and feel like you're young again.

Why Is Weight Loss So Difficult After 60?

Although many people begin to experience this annoyance around the age of 60, losing weight and keeping it off can become a problem as early as 50. What is happening?

Your metabolism is slowing down as a result of hormones. To begin with, as you become older, your metabolism decreases.

Robert Herbst on Losing Weight After 60: Powerlifting expert and 19-time World Champion Robert Herbst says, "Loss of muscle mass results from decreased testosterone and human growth hormone (HGH) synthesis, which slows metabolism".

Carolyn Dean on Dieting After 60: Dr. Carolyn Dean, an author of many books about women's health, says, "Your efforts to lose weight are hampered because the loss of nutrients like magnesium has diminished the production of hormones that increase metabolism." In essence, you are not to blame for this. Age-related declines in your body's ability to produce essential hormones make weight loss a challenge. Perimenopause and menopause are common conditions for women in their 50s and 60s. You burn fewer calories due to this change than you previously did.

Jill McKay on Over 60 Diet and Exercise: "Our body temperature would change during menstruation, which would result in an extra 300 calories burned each month, says Jill McKay, a certified personal trainer, and group fitness instructor. Although it's not much, over time, it adds up. Insulin resistance is a problem that occurs throughout both perimenopause and menopause and makes it increasingly harder to lose weight". This means that you can no longer consume the foods you used to! This also applies to portions; you might discover that you can no longer consume as much as you formerly could without putting on weight.

Potential Health Conditions to Be Aware Of

Most people find it difficult to lose weight beyond age 60, although this is normal. If, however, you are having difficulty losing weight, you might want to consult your doctor to ensure you are healthy. The two most frequent medical problems that might result in weight gain are 1) the thyroid losing function and 2) insulin becoming less effective. If you can effectively metabolize your sugars, you can tell by the hemoglobin A1c test that is commonly administered. If not, diabetes could be a possibility for you. These disorders are especially prevalent in women approaching menopause.

9 Practical Ways for Weight Loss After 60

So many men and women struggle with weight loss after age 60. To tip the scales in your favor, there are several techniques for shedding that weight.

1. Strength Training: Resistance training, often known as strength training, isn't typically the first exercise older adults choose. The most popular workouts are often cardio exercises like treadmill walking or elliptical.

Carol Michaels on healthy eating after 60

Carol Michaels, an Idea Fitness Trainer, is concerned that many seniors are overlooking the benefits of strength training. Strength training is often the exercise component that's missing in weight loss programs for those over 60. This workout strengthens and develops muscle using weights (or your body weight). It strengthens muscle fibers and fortifies tendons, bones, and ligaments. We lose muscle mass as we age, primarily due to our slowing metabolisms. This leads to an even slower metabolism. Strength training, however, may break that pattern of muscle loss; it can reverse muscle loss at any age. "Muscle is metabolically active; therefore, the more muscle mass you have, the quicker your metabolism," Carol explains. Strength training can therefore aid with weight reduction.

DO I USE FREE WEIGHTS OR MACHINES?

Now that we are all in agreement that strength training is fantastic, you may ask how to do this. Many older adults, Carol claims, are in their mid-60s and have no idea where to start. Should you utilize the equipment at the gym? While machines can be useful for people who have balance concerns, free weight exercise has several advantages. You can strength train at home with free weights and improve by one-pound increments. Using free weights teaches you how to move your body naturally throughout daily tasks. You can build more main muscle groups using free weights instead of a machine because you won't rely on them for support. Weight machines only work for large muscle groups. They can overlook the little but crucial stabilizer muscles that provide balance, coordination, and injury avoidance.

DO I NEED TO STRENGTH TRAIN REGULARLY?

You don't have to strength train like a madman to reap the rewards. Carol advises setting a goal of twice weekly. "Build up each muscle group, switching between your upper and lower body. To avoid creating imbalances, work the front, rear, and sides of the body. If you're over 60 and new to fitness, you could begin with a very light weight".

Strength training after 60

After you've scheduled your workouts, Carol advises performing the exercise 5–10 times. You should feel the muscle working around the fifth to eighth repetition. You should feel like you've exercised the muscle by the last repetition but not exhausted. If you are too tired, you are doing too much weight. Many professionals online offer strength training plans with pictures and instructions, but you can talk with a gym to have a personal trainer show you what exercises to do.

2. Keep Carbs and Sugars Low

Even if you've never had a problem with delicious desserts and carb-heavy meals, dieting after 60 might be challenging because your body may start to change. Even if you've maintained your weight for years, one simple dessert can make you gain weight. The larger issue, however, is that older persons over 60 have a propensity for increased blood sugar because of insulin resistance.

Denny Hemingson on Losing Weight After Age 60

Functional Diagnostic Nutrition Practitioner Denny Hemingson, 61, explains that insulin tells the liver, muscles, and fat cells to absorb glucose from the bloodstream. When such cells develop insulin resistance, glucose is not used and stays in the blood, leading to excessive blood sugar levels. Eventually, this leads to metabolic syndrome, type 2 diabetes, and pre-diabetes. In this situation, the body finds it considerably more difficult to shed additional pounds. The solution? Reducing carbohydrates. Cutting carbs will lower your blood sugar, making it easier to keep a healthy weight. The Keto diet is supported by Carolyn Dean. This enables the body to burn down its glycogen reserves of sugar from carbohydrates before activating fat burning to use the remaining fat cells as energy. Although the ketogenic diet is steadily becoming more well-known in the health and fitness world as a means to burn fat more quickly than ever before, you are advised to see your doctor first. According to Carolyn, the Keto diet aims to limit your daily carb intake to 20–50 grams.

3. Drink Half Your Body Weight In Ounces of Water

Although drinking water doesn't in itself aid in weight loss, it's a fact that many individuals mistake thirst for hunger. The cure? Drink a ton of water. You should consume half your body weight in ounces of water.

4. Consider Adding Magnesium to Your Diet

You might not have considered including magnesium in your diet. Magnesium aids in synthesizing proteins, carbohydrates, and fats and boosts weight reduction and metabolism. You may easily add magnesium to your water to add it to your diet. Add sea salt and an absorbable type of magnesium to your water, such as magnesium citrate powder, advises Carolyn. This will make sticking to a low-carb diet much simpler and prevent you from experiencing the energy loss, sluggishness, and headaches brought on by electrolyte loss. Another thing to consider is that since sugar depletes magnesium and strains the body, avoiding it can help counteract the effects of stress.

5. Get Some Sun

Don't get sunburn or anything, but please take vitamin D! If you don't get enough vitamin D, you might reach for more food than you need. Leptin and vitamin D work together to control hunger signals, according to Denny. This mechanism breaks down when vitamin D levels are low, which makes people overeat. You can get the Vitamin D you need by getting more sun. Go outside, enjoy the weather, and celebrate your ability to restrain your appetite!

6. Reduce Stress Through Yoga

Relaxing is an excellent approach to handling stress. And occasionally, you require some encouragement. Yoga, which does more than merely reduce stress, is suggested by Denny. Your balance, core strength, and awareness will all increase. Consider using meditation, prayer, and nature walks as additional stress-reduction techniques.

7. Get Quality Sleep

The impact of sleep on your general health is incredible.

You will have greater energy for your strength training session, and your body also creates human growth hormones while you sleep (HGH). Denny suggests obtaining 7-8 hours of good sleep every night. The greatest way to ensure that you get a good night's sleep is to:

- Establish a regular bedtime habit by going to bed simultaneously every day.
- Avoid using a screen before bed (smartphones, computers, TVs).

So don't skimp on sleep—it keeps you young!

8. Consider Meal Prepping

Meal planning can make you eat healthier throughout the week. Stop consuming manufactured food, Jill advises. Consider meal planning for the week so you can prepare larger portions and divide them into smaller meals throughout the week.

9. Don't Push Yourself Too Hard

Lastly, try not to be so hard on yourself. If a week passes without you dropping a pound, don't worry! That could be completely typical. According to our experts, you shouldn't drastically reduce your calorie consumption. Don't substantially reduce your calorie intake, Jill advises.

"Adequate calories are vital! Muscle loss brought on by rapid weight reduction alters body composition and may impede metabolism. In other words, if you aren't eating enough, all of your strength training success might be undone. Last but not least, don't overwork yourself at the gym. That's not necessary at all! If you need a break, take one! If you feel the weight is too much, lighten up! The goal isn't to make yourself miserable but to maintain your health.

Ketogenic Diet And Menopause

Menopause is the stage when a woman's menstrual period ends for 12 months in a row. It signals the end of her reproductive and fertile years. Common side effects of changing hormone levels during menopause include mood changes, hot flashes, and sleep disruption. Following menopause, many women also suffer an average weight increase of roughly five pounds. Some people suggest the keto diet, which has a very low carbohydrate intake and a high-fat content, to reduce menopausal symptoms and maintain hormonal balance. However, because it might have unfavorable side effects, it might not be the ideal strategy for all women. This chapter explores how several hormones might change while someone is in ketosis. It also looks at the possible advantages of this diet for menopausal women.

Keto and Hormones

Hormonal imbalances, particularly those involving estrogen and progesterone, can result during menopause. This can cause lower metabolism and decreased insulin sensitivity. Additionally, it could cause an increase in food cravings. There isn't much proof that the ketogenic diet can affect the ratio of reproductive hormones. However, the keto diet can significantly regulate the balance of certain hormones that affect insulin production and appetite management.

Benefits

Here are some potential benefits of the ketogenic diet for menopausal women.

Effect on Insulin Sensitivity: Insulin is a hormone that aids in transferring glucose (sugar) from your bloodstream into your cells to be utilized as an energy source. Hot flashes and night sweats, two symptoms of menopause, have also been shown to be significantly correlated with insulin resistance. Your body's cells develop insulin resistance when they don't react well to the hormone. This increases the amount of glucose circulating in your blood and increases your chance of developing a chronic disease. According to several research, the ketogenic diet may help persons with diabetes improve their insulin sensitivity, have lower insulin levels, and use fewer drugs to achieve their goal blood sugar levels. Additionally, one research tested the ketogenic diet on those with endometrial or ovarian cancer. According to the research, following the ketogenic diet for 12 weeks resulted in greater reductions in belly fat and increases in insulin sensitivity.

Effect on Weight Gain: People who are overweight or obese have been proven to benefit from the keto diet in terms of weight reduction, lipid profiles, and glycemic management. In one research, postmenopausal women examined four food regimens to determine which was most effective for maintaining weight. Researchers compared the Mediterranean diet to a low-fat, low-carb diet in line with the current Dietary Guidelines for Americans in the United States. At the study's conclusion, researchers discovered that those who consumed a diet low in carbohydrates, high in protein, and moderate in fat had a lower risk of weight gain. A low-fat diet, however, increased the likelihood of postmenopausal weight gain the most. It's crucial to note that the reduced-carb diet used in this study typically had 163 grams of carbs, which is significantly more than what is advised for a keto diet.

There aren't many studies linking the ketogenic diet to menopausal-related weight gain.

Effect on Food Cravings: Many women report having more appetite and cravings throughout the menopausal transition and the postmenopausal years. It has been shown that the ketogenic diet increases feelings of fullness. For instance, one set of research indicates that being in ketosis may cause a decrease in hunger. This could be because of diets with a lot of protein and fat increase satiety through various mechanisms. This includes decreasing intestinal transit, decreasing gastric emptying, and playing a role in releasing hunger hormones. Another research examined 20 obese people to evaluate their dietary desires, sleep patterns, sexual activity, and general quality of life while adhering to a very low-calorie ketogenic diet. Researchers discovered that patients experienced improvements in their sexual function, good eating management, significant weight reduction, and overall quality of life.

Side Effects
The keto diet may offer some advantages for menopause, but it is not for everyone. The "keto flu" is a common group of side effects that you may experience after beginning the keto diet. This is because switching to a very low carbohydrate diet requires some time for your body to adjust. The following symptoms are linked to the keto flu:

- Brain fog
- Headache
- Body aches
- Feeling faint
- Stomach pain/discomfort
- Dizziness
- Sore throat
- Flu-like symptoms
- Fatigue
- Nausea
- Heartbeat changes

When the diet is carefully followed, symptoms often peak in the first week and progressively subside during the next three weeks. The negative effects that the keto diet could have on your general heart health are another issue. A few studies have suggested that a ketogenic diet's high quantities of saturated fat might raise the levels of bad cholesterol in our bodies. Diets high in fat have also been linked with inflammation and the disruption of gut microbiota (bacteria in the digestive system). Additionally, some people are concerned about the rigorous restriction on carbs, usually less than 50 grams. This is so because many items high in carbohydrates prohibited by the keto diet are also high in nutrients, including fiber, vitamins, and minerals. If you don't take the right supplements, you might be at risk for vitamin shortages. Menopause may be frustrating and difficult for some women, as can the time immediately after menopause. Know that you are not alone. Menopause-related weight gain can be lessened by adopting good eating habits and frequent exercise routines.

Although the keto diet may help some people's symptoms, it's not a one-size-fits-all solution. Finding out which eating strategy will work best for you requires a conversation with your healthcare physician and a qualified dietitian.

Mistakes Beginners Make and How to Avoid Them

Given the paucity of data on the ketogenic diet, it might be difficult to predict whether or not you will have any specific effects, such as weight reduction. It can be challenging to follow the keto diet "properly" because it is so severely restrictive. For instance, you'll have to forgo starchy vegetables, limit fruits, and avoid grains, sauces, juice, and sweets on this diet. Moreover, as per the standard keto food list, you must consume a lot of fats (lots of them). By doing this, you'll enter the metabolic state of ketosis, which causes your body to burn fat instead of carbs, potentially increasing your weight loss. However, because fats exist in various forms (not all healthy) and carbohydrates are present in almost everything, it may be easy to err here, especially if you're new to the keto diet.

To ensure you're using this technique as safely as possible, avoid the following common keto pitfalls:

1. Cutting Your Carbs and Increasing Your Fat Too Much Too Quickly. You might be eating cereal, sandwiches, and spaghetti one day and then decide to start the keto diet and limit your daily carbohydrate intake to 20 grams (g), which is usually the suggested starting point. (For reference, a medium apple provides 25 g of carbohydrates.) That can be a major adjustment for your body. Consider easing in. According to Lara Clevenger, a ketogenic dietitian-nutritionist, "before starting a keto diet, individuals may benefit from weaning down their carbohydrate consumption instead of reducing carbohydrates cold turkey."

2. Not Drinking Enough Water on Keto: On a ketogenic diet, dehydration is more likely to occur. "Your fluid and electrolyte balance may change due to the ketogenic diet's significant reduction in carbohydrate intake". According to nutrition manager Alyssa Tucci "carbs are stored in the body together with water, so when these reserves are depleted, that water is lost along with them. She further claims that the removal of the accumulated ketones in urine by the body depletes it of salt and water. All that to say: Drink up. All of this to say: Cheers! To meet the recommendation of drinking half your body weight in ounces of water each day, Tucci advises waking up to a large glass of water and sipping on it frequently throughout the day.

3. Failing to prepare for the keto flu: During the first two weeks of the keto diet, you may suffer what is known as the "keto flu," or flu-like symptoms (such as muscular cramps, nausea, pains, and exhaustion), as your body switches from being a carbohydrate burner to a fat burner. Please note that not everyone experiences it. If you're not ready for this feeling, you could assume something is wrong and stop your diet altogether. More than that, according to Clevenger, planning your meals or meal preparation can help you get through the low-energy phase of the transition. She also suggests drinking plenty of water, consuming meals high in potassium, magnesium, and sodium, and other measures to deal with keto flu symptoms.

4. Forgetting to Consume Omega-3 Fatty Acid-Rich Foods: Don't limit yourself to bacon, cheese, and cream, even if fat is the main component of the diet. Aim to consume more anti-inflammatory omega-3 fatty acids, especially EPA and DHA, which are present in foods like salmon, herring, sardines, oysters, and mussels, adds Clevenger. (If seafood isn't your thing, try krill oil or cod liver oil.) If you haven't loaded up on avocado, olive oil, and seeds like chia and flaxseed, do so. Other healthy fats are also a wonderful option. Not only are they keto-friendly, but they also provide the beneficial polyunsaturated and monounsaturated fats your body needs to function at its peak.

5. Not adding enough salt to your food: Given that people consume more sodium than ever in a diet high in processed foods, you probably aren't used to hearing the recommendation to consume more salt. However, it's essential for keto. Not only does the body lose sodium when ketones are cleared from the body, but you may also consume significantly less table salt now that you've eliminated the main source of salt in the typical American diet: packaged, processed foods like bread, crackers, cookies, and chips. Table salt is made up of 40% sodium and 60% chloride. "If you're on a ketogenic diet, chances are you'll need to make most, if not all, of your meals and snacks from scratch, so simply season with salt," Tucci advises.

6. Going It Alone and Not Clearing the Diet With Your Doc: Many people try the ketogenic diet, hoping it will treat a medical condition. If that is you, Clevenger advises that you first consult your physician to get their approval of your plan, particularly if you are also on medication. As your signs and symptoms improve, your doctor may need to change certain drugs," she adds.

7. Ignoring your intake of vegetables: Veggies contain carbs. You must thus be careful with how much food you consume, even lettuce. You risk consuming too many carbohydrates if you're careless or eating them randomly, which will cause you to exit ketosis. On the other hand, if keeping track of every small carrot becomes too challenging, you may skip vegetables altogether. But while watching amounts and properly tracking carbohydrates, it's vital to include veggies because they contain fiber that helps avoid constipation, a possible side effect of the keto diet. Choose nonstarchy foods for a range of nutrients, advises Tucci, like leafy greens, broccoli, cauliflower, cucumber, tomato, asparagus, and bell peppers.

8. Getting Obsessed with Carb Counting and Ignoring the Importance of Food Quality: When significantly reducing carbohydrates seems to be the only purpose of the keto diet, everything else may seem like an afterthought. "Reducing your carbohydrate consumption is important, but when finances allow, focusing on higher-quality items can help enhance your health, too," claims Clevenger. This entails choosing foods high in omega 3, such as wild salmon, organic meats, or grass-fed, local, and choosing whole foods for snacks rather than prepared keto-friendly items. It also involves including as many nutrient-dense fruits and vegetables in your diet as you can to maintain a balanced diet. Many qualified dietitians aren't fans of the keto diet because it could result in dietary deficits. You can prevent these by working with an RD personally as you follow the keto diet.

CHAPTER 3: Keto And Exercise

Before you begin combining keto with exercise, there are a few key points that experts want you to be aware of. You've heard of the ketogenic (also known as the keto) diet by now; you know, the one that pushes you to consume a lot of healthy fats while largely avoiding carbohydrates. The keto diet has entered the mainstream and is especially well-liked by the fitness crowd. While it's true that it may have some performance advantages, doctors say there are certain crucial facts you should be aware of if you're considering going out while on the ketogenic diet. At first, you might not feel so great, and not feeling your best might affect your workouts. Ramsey Bergeron, a keto athlete and NASM-certified personal trainer in Scottsdale, Arizona, says the first few days may seem like you're in a fog. "Your brain uses glucose (from carbohydrates) as its main energy source, so switching to ketone bodies produced by the liver's breakdown of fats would require some getting used to". Fortunately, the mental fog usually fades after a few days. Bergeron advises against exercising in dangerous situations that call for rapid reactions, such as riding a bike on the road with cars. It's not a good idea to undertake a new workout during the first few weeks of a keto diet. Bergeron advises, "Keep doing what you are doing." This is mainly due to the first point: most people don't first feel great on keto. When extreme, this initial unpleasant phase—which typically passes within a few days to a couple of weeks—can be referred to as the "keto flu" due to its flu-like grogginess and gastrointestinal disturbances. When my clients try anything new, I always advise them to keep the variables to a minimum," says Bergeron. "You won't know what worked and what didn't if you alter too many things at once," he continues.

It's essential that you eat enough before exercising while following a ketogenic diet.
"Make sure you're providing your body with enough energy, and avoid decreasing calories too strictly," advises nutritionist Lisa Booth. This is significant because, according to her, people on the keto diet tend to undereat. According to Booth, a keto diet also has an appetite-suppressing effect, so you can think you're not hungry even if you aren't providing your body with enough energy. "When you restrict an entire food category (in this case, carbohydrates), you often automatically decrease calories," she adds. You'll feel awful if you drastically cut calories while working out, which might affect your performance and results.

Low- and moderate-intensity workouts can help you burn more fat.
This is one of the key arguments favoring keto for weight reduction. "When you're in ketosis, you don't use glycogen as an energy source," says Booth. "Glycogen is a substance stored in muscles and tissues as a reserve of carbs. Instead, you're using ketone bodies and fat. A ketogenic diet can help enhance fat oxidation, spare glycogen, produce less lactate, and use less oxygen if you engage in aerobic workouts like biking or running," she clarifies. Booth continues, "But it probably won't improve performance". Furthermore, while following a ketogenic diet, you don't have to exert yourself to the fullest. According to Chelsea Axe, a certified strength, and conditioning specialist in Nashville, "Studies have indicated that ketogenic diets combined with moderate-intensity exercise can favorably impact one's body composition.

Research has shown that ketogenic diets increase the body's capacity to burn fat both at rest and during low- to moderate-intensities, so your weight-loss efforts may be optimized when exercising in these zones," she says.

High-intensity exercises may be best avoided while on a diet.

According to Axe, studies have shown that diets heavy in a certain macronutrient, such as fat, encourage a greater capacity to use that macronutrient as fuel. However, she says, "regardless of your macronutrient ratio consumption, the body adjusts to using glycogen as fuel during high-intensity activity. You'll recall from earlier that carbs fuel glycogen stores, so if you don't consume a lot of them, your ability to execute higher-intensity exercise can be compromised. Instead, Axe argues that moderate exercise is best for maximizing the body's capacity to burn fat. As a result, those who participate in intense exercises like CrossFit or HIIT might benefit more from adopting a ketogenic diet during their off-season or when they are less concerned with their performance.

To profit from your workouts, you need to eat adequate fat.

This is essential; otherwise, you risk losing out on all the advantages and having your performance deteriorate. According to Bergeron, if you follow a ketogenic diet but don't consume enough fats, you are effectively following an Atkins diet with high protein, low carbs, and low fat. He says that doing so might make you incredibly hungry, reduce muscle mass, and be almost impossible to maintain. Most low-carb diets have a bad reputation for a reason. You're likely to experience fatigue and lose out on entering ketosis if you don't consume enough fat to make up for the carbs you're missing. According to Bergeron, most calories must come from good fat sources like fish, grass-fed meats, coconut oil, and avocado.

When combining diet with exercise, paying attention to your body is important.

This is true throughout your whole experience, but particularly in the first few weeks, you follow a ketogenic diet. According to Booth, "if you often feel tired, lightheaded, or drained, your body may not function properly on a very low-carb diet. "The most crucial factor should be your health and wellbeing. See how you feel after adding more carbohydrates. If this makes you feel better, the ketogenic diet might not be the best option for you," she suggests.

Keto-Friendly Drinks

Yes, they exist.

What makes a drink keto?

Because the keto diet calls for getting fewer than 10% of your daily calories from carbs—roughly 20 to 30 grams a day—you should avoid drinks that exceed, or even better, fall well below, that percentage. Why? With very few exceptions, you don't want to consume all of your daily carbohydrate allowance in a single serving. When searching for keto-friendly options, look for beverages with less than 5 grams of carbohydrates on the nutrition label. Avoid heavily sweetened beverages (sorry, orange juice fans) or include additional sweeteners, which, regrettably, include most cocktails.

What beverages work best for a keto diet?

We searched for the most acclaimed and highly rated keto-friendly beverages for this list. Some choices are apparent (hello, number one), while others will have you rushing to Starbucks to get every keto-friendly beverage they offer. To ensure that you don't feel like you are missing out on anything, we have also provided several alcoholic alternatives and soda substitutes. Before beginning the keto diet, consult a nutritionist and/or a doctor to ensure you're obtaining all the necessary nutrients. Do whatever seems right for you as well! All bodies are different.

Water

Yes, of course, we do. But water satisfies a keto-friendly substance's fundamental and most important condition: it contains little carbohydrates. Craig Clarke says on the keto site Ruled.me, "During the first few days of carbohydrate restriction, the body normally eliminates water and minerals at an accelerated pace. A few days later, when ketone levels rise, even more water than usual will be expelled." So drink up!

Sparkling Water

According to the aforementioned logcv, all zero-calorie seltzers are also keto.

That means quitting your favorite La Croix habit won't be necessary if you go keto. The Sparkling Ice waters are also a favorite among many keto dieters. This Amazon reviewer wrote, "I'm on the keto diet and drink them constantly while still losing weight. They have a terrific flavor and satisfy my thirst. Additionally, each bottle has 0 calories and 0 or 5 carbohydrates."

Zevia Zero Calorie Soda

This keto-friendly Tiktok designer vouch for Zevia, saying, "If you are a soda-holic, Zevia is a wonderful solution to replace all that soda." Amazon shoppers adore it as a soda substitute because it contains neither calories nor sugar. Most diet sodas are also OK when following a ketogenic diet.

Green Tea

While on the keto diet, remember your body's other health requirements! Green tea adheres to the diet while providing much-needed antioxidants and minerals. Matcha powder is also included in this. According to Carine Claudepierre of the keto-focused SweetAsHoney blog, the ingredient comprises dried green tea leaves that have been crushed into green tea powder. It is carb-free and keto-friendly.

Black Tea

Black tea has no net carbohydrates, although heavy cream can be added for taste if desired, which is, in fact, keto-friendly. Tea is a good keto-friendly beverage because it's a perfect substitute for water and can be served hot or cold, according to the MunchMunchYum blog.

Bulletproof Coffee

Yes, you can drink your coffee black, but adding that sweet, sweet (but low-carb, high-fat) butter can help you reach your calorie targets much more quickly. According to a blog article by WholesomeYum's Maya Krampf, "Bulletproof coffee is coffee brewed with either butter or ghee AND coconut oil or MCT oil. My favorite part is the extra energy I got from combining butter and MCT oil with my coffee. I usually feel satisfied after eating it and am attentive and productive."

Non-Dairy Milk Alternatives

Protein. Fat. Little carbohydrates. Everything is fine. Almond milk, according to Elana Amsterdam of Elana's Pantry, is the greatest milk for the keto diet. It has amazing flavor and mouthfeel and is relatively low in carbohydrates, making it my favorite."

Protein Shakes

Now that everyone is interested in going keto, several protein powders are made expressly for the keto diet. You may either make your own or choose an Atkins-style shake. It has almost 23,000 five-star ratings on Amazon, and one reviewer claimed that it doesn't taste like "a 'diet' item". "I use this to satisfy my weet tooth craving while on the keto diet."

Hard Liquor

The blog Green and Keto claimed that "alcohols like vodka, scotch, rum, whiskey, gin, and tequila are great options on the keto diet. They have no carbohydrates or sugar when eaten alone". Just be careful not to combine them with any liquids or calorie sweeteners. Your best friends in keto mixers are sugar-free sodas, seltzers, and tonics.

Starbucks' Peach Citrus White Tea

After the drink became quite popular, there was considerable disagreement about whether it was keto-friendly, but in reality, it is. Only Starbucks' unsweetened Peach Citrus White Tea, heavy cream, two to four pumps of sugar-free vanilla syrup, and ice are combined to make it.

Starbucks Pink Drink

The OG Pink Drink wasn't originally keto, but early adopters of the diet quickly figured out how to make it such. To give this drink a keto makeover, request a sugar-free syrup, unsweetened Passion Tango tea, and light or heavy creamer. "Grammable keto," boom. This TikTok creator said, "It is one of my favorite clean keto Starbucks beverages.

Lagunitas Daytime IPA

This beer has an ABV of 4%, fewer than 100 calories, and 3 grams carbohydrates. This indicates that it is keto-friendly, and the designer of the keto Tiktok claims that it has a "cool name" and "tastes amazing."

Michelob Ultra Beer

"Michelob Ultra is below 3 g carbs per serving and has 95 calories," Joe Duff of The Diet Chef wrote in a blog post. "It has a refreshing flavor with a little bit of sweetness."

CHAPTER 4: Recipes

Breakfast

1. Banana Keto Chia Pudding

Servings: 1 **Preparation time:** 130 minutes
Ingredients
- White Yoghurt - 2 tablespoons
- Chia seeds - 1, 5 tbsp
- KetoDiet protein drink banana flavor - 1
- Milk - 150 ml

Instructions
Mix all the ingredients together, pour the mixture into a glass and let it solidify in the refrigerator for at least 2 hours. Decorate with a sprig of mint, for example.

2. Green Keto Smoothie

Servings: 1 **Preparation time:** 15 minutes
Ingredients
- Fresh baby spinach - 30 g
- Apple - 1/2 pcs
- KetoDiet Protein Drink - 1 serving
- Coconut milk - 200 ml
- Young barley - 1 teaspoon
- Water - 100 ml

Instructions
Pour the milk into a blender, add sliced apple, baby spinach, water, protein drink, and young barley and mix all the ingredients thoroughly.

Garnish the smoothie with a slice of lemon and serve.

3. Matcha Keto Pudding

Servings: 1 Preparations: 60 minutes
Ingredients

- Matcha tea - 1 teaspoon
- Chia seeds - 20 g
- KetoDiet protein panna cotta - 1 serving
- Almond milk - 100 ml
- Nuts mix for decoration
- Vanilla essence according to taste

Instructions

Mix the powder from the protein panny cotty bag and matcha tea into the almond milk, add the chia seeds, and mix the vanilla essence. Pour into a bowl and let it solidify in the refrigerator for at least 45 minutes. Garnish the protein matcha pudding with chopped nuts and serve.

4. Keto Waffles with Chocolate Cottage Cheese

Servings: 2 Preparation time: 30 minutes
Ingredients

- Cocoa - 1 tbsp
- KetoDiet Protein drink hazelnut flavor and chocolate - 1 tbsp
- KetoDiet Protein drink creamy without flavor - 2 measuring cups

- Baking powder - 1/4 teaspoon
- Almond flour - 30 g
- Butter - 40 g
- Milk - 120 ml
- Whole cottage cheese - 1 piece
- Cinnamon - 1/2 teaspoon
- Vanilla essence according to taste
- Egg - 2 pcs

Instructions

Prepare the dough for 6 waffles. In a bowl, mix almond flour, KetoDiet protein powder, baking powder, cinnamon, add eggs, milk, warmed butter, vanilla extract, and whip everything into a smooth dough. We can use a stick mixer. Pour the dough into a warm waffle maker and bake until pink. Meanwhile, whip the cottage cheese with cocoa and season with a spoonful protein drink hazelnut and chocolate. Finished waffles are served with whipped chocolate curd.

5. Cheese Keto Patties

Servings: 2 **Preparation time:** 30 minutes
Ingredients
- Basil according to taste
- Herbs according to taste
- Cheddar - 2 slices
- Cherry tomatoes - 5 pcs
- KetoDiet protein omelet with cheese flavor - 1 bag
- Cauliflower - 300 g
- Olive oil according to taste
- Parmesan - 50 g
- Salt according to taste

Instructions

Salt the grated cauliflower, let it stand and drain the excess water and squeeze through a cloth. Thoroughly mix one serving of KetoDiet protein omelet (in a shaker or whisk) in 100 ml of water, mix with cauliflower, herbs, and grated Parmesan cheese. From the dough, we make patties, which we fry in a pan until browned; we put a cheddar slice and let it melt. We serve vegetable salads with pancakes, for example from cherry tomatoes with basil dripped with olive oil.

6. Keto Porridge with Wild Berries

Servings: 1 **Preparation time:** 15 minutes
Ingredients
- chicory syrup according to taste
- KetoDiet raspberry porridge - 1 piece
- Coconut milk - 50 ml
- Forest fruit - 100 g

- Milk - 100 ml
- Almond slices - 1 tbsp
- Shredded coconut - 1 tbsp
- Cottage cheese - 1 tbsp

Instructions

Whip the protein raspberry porridge with the milk (cow and coconut) until smooth and put it in the microwave for a minute, or heat the milk in a saucepan and pour the contents of the bag into the hot milk and mix thoroughly. Stir 50 g of mixed forest fruit into the finished porridge, add coconut, a spoonful of cottage cheese and garnish with dry roasted almond slices and the remaining fruit.

7. Keto Potato Pancakes

Servings: 1 **Preparation time:** 20 minutes

Ingredients
- Balsamic - 1 teaspoon (for salad)
- Celery - 150 g
- Garlic - 1 clove
- Crushed cumin according to taste
- KetoDiet protein pancake with garlic flavor - 1 serving
- Marjoram according to taste
- Ground flax seeds - 1 tablespoon
- Oil according to taste
- Olive oil - 1 tablespoon (for salad)
- Pepper according to taste
- Radish - 3 pcs (for salad)
- A mixture of green salads (arugula, romaine lettuce, corn salad)1 handful (for salad)
- Salt according to taste
- Water - 100 ml

Instructions

Grate the celery and mix it with all the ingredients, including the protein pancake powder, to make a thinner dough. We make patties from the dough, which we fry until golden in a pan.
Serve with a vegetable salad of mixed salad (we used corn on the cob, arugula, beet leaves), chopped radishes, which we cut. Mix everything and drizzle with the prepared dressing of olive oil and balsamic.

8. Baked Avocado

Servings: 2 **Preparation time:** 30 minutes

Ingredients
- Avocado - 2
- Cherry tomatoes to taste
- Pepper to taste

- Bacon - 4 slices
- Salt to taste
- Cottage cheese - 1
- Egg - 4 pieces

Instructions

Cut the avocado lengthwise and remove the stone.

We dig out a little pulp with a spoon. Put the hollowed-out avocados in a small baking dish with baking paper. Tap 1 small egg in each half of the avocado and add a piece of bacon, cottage cheese, cherry tomatoes, etc. Add salt and pepper. Bake until the egg is ready.

9. Pasta Salad

Servings: 1 **Preparation time:** 20 minutes
Ingredients

- KetoDiet protein pasta Fusilli- 1 serving
- Olive oil - 2 tablespoons (for mayonnaise)
- Pepper according to taste
- Radish - 3 pcs
- Cucumber - 100 g
- A mixture of green salads (arugula, romaine lettuce, corn salad)1 handful
- Salt according to taste
- Sour cream - 1 tablespoon (for mayonnaise)
- Green pepper - 100 g

Instructions

Cut peppers, cucumber, and radish and mix them with salad and ready-made protein pasta, which we cooked according to the instructions. Pour the homemade mayonnaise over the salad, which we prepare from sour cream, olive oil, salt, and pepper. Garnish with chives or herbs and serve.

ATTENTION! If you have this mayonnaise in step 1 of your diet plan, omit half the amount (= 1 DCL) of milk allowed that day.

10. Baked Keto Peppers

Servings: 2 **Preparation time:** 60 minutes
Ingredients

- Balsamic - 1 teaspoon (for salad)
- White or green pepper - 2 pcs
- Garlic - 1 clove
- Cherry tomatoes - 5 pcs (for salad)
- Half onion
- KetoDiet protein omelet with cheese flavor - 1 piece
- Ground beef meat - 100 g
- Olive oil - 20 ml for peppers + to taste for salad

- Pepper according to taste
- Radish - 5 pcs (for salad)
- Rosemary according to taste
- A mixture of green salads (arugula, romaine lettuce, corn salad), a handful (for salad)
- Salt according to taste
- Water - 100 ml
- Mushrooms - 3 pcs

Instructions

We clean the pepper, cut it in half, and get rid of the kernels. Fry the sliced mushrooms with a sprig of rosemary in a hot pan and set them aside. Now fry the chopped onion, add the minced meat, garlic and season with pepper and salt. Once the meat is roasted, add the mushrooms to the mixture and mix. Fill the halved peppers with the meat mixture and pour them over the water with a mixed protein omelet—Bake in a baking dish at 150 ° C for about 20 minutes. Serve with a vegetable salad of 5 cherry tomatoes, 5 radishes, and a handful of mixed salad, which we drizzle with a dressing of olive oil, and balsamic, salt and pepper.

11. Easter Lamb

Servings: 6 **Preparation time:** 0 minutes
Ingredients
- Chicory syrup - 1/4 cup
- 1/2 lemon juice
- KetoDiet Protein Drink - 1 serving
- Baking powder - 1 piece
- Almond flour - 1 and 1/4 cup
- Ground flax seeds - half cup
- Ground poppy seeds - 1/2 cup
- Greek white yogurt - 1 mug
- Egg - 4 pieces

Instructions

Mix Greek yogurt, add almond flour, 1 serving of protein drink, eggs, mixed flax seeds, poppy seeds, lemon juice, chicory syrup, and 1 baking powder. Mix everything well and pour into the erased form—Bake for about 40 minutes at 180 ° C.

12. Keto Tart with Wild Berries

Servings: 2 **Preparation:** 60 minutes
Ingredients
- Chicory syrup - 1 tablespoon
- KetoDiet protein panna cotta - 1 serving
- Forest fruit - 200 g
- Mascarpone - 100 g
- Mint for decoration

- Whole cottage cheese - 100 g
- Gelatin - 1 piece

Instructions

Mix mascarpone with cottage cheese and protein panna cotta mixture and sweeten with chicory syrup. Pour the finished cream into a bowl and place the forest fruits on top. Pour the prepared gelatin according to the instructions and let it cool in the refrigerator until the gelatin hardens. Decorate with a sprig of mint, for example.

Lunch

1. Keto Pasta Curry

Servings: 2 Preparation time: 30 minutes
Ingredients

- Fresh baby spinach a handful of petals
- Fresh coriander according to taste
- Garlic - 1 clove
- Zucchini - 100 g
- Curry spice according to taste
- KetoDiet protein cheese soup with vegetables - 1 bag
- KetoDiet protein pasta Fusilli - 1 bag
- Coconut milk - 50 ml
- Oil according to taste
- Shallot - 1
- Water - 170 ml

Instructions

Fry finely chopped onion, crushed garlic, chopped zucchini, and curry in oil and sauté until soft. Mix KetoDiet protein cheese soup in hot water, add to the mixture and cook for a while. Mix with Fusilli protein pasta cooked according to the instructions, spinach, pour coconut milk and sprinkle with coriander.

2. Vegetable-Mushroom Keto Omelette

Serving: 1 **Preparation time:** 20 minutes
Ingredients

- Fresh baby spinach, a handful of petals
- Zucchini -100 g
- Pumpkin - 100 g
- KetoDiet Protein omelet with bacon flavor - 1 serving
- Oil according to taste
- Parmesanfor sprinkling

- Pepper according to taste
- Salt according to taste
- Mushrooms - 50 g

Instructions

Cut zucchini, pumpkin, and mushrooms into pieces, fry in oil, salt, pepper, add spinach leaves. Mix the KetoDiet protein omelet in water, pour over the vegetables, sprinkle with cheese, and bake for 5-10 minutes at 180 ° C.

3. Avocado Foam

Serving: 1 **Preparation time:** 15 min
Ingredients
- Avocado - 1/2
- Cocoa - 2 tablespoons
- Coconut milk - 20 ml
- KetoDiet protein drink flavored with hazelnut and chocolate - 10 g
- Shredded coconut - 1 tbsp

Instructions

Dissolve one tablespoon (10 g) of flavored protein drink (vanilla or hazelnut flavor and chocolate) in coconut milk, add skinless and stone-free avocado, cocoa and mix into a smooth cream. Serve sprinkled with grated coconut.

4. Keto Specle with Spinach

Servings: 2 **Preparation:** 30 minutes
Ingredients
- Fresh baby spinach handful
- Garlic - 1 clove
- KetoDiet protein omelet with cheese flavor - 1 bag
- Baking powder - 1/2 teaspoon
- Olive oil according to taste
- Parmesan - 25 g
- Shallot - 1/2
- Whipping cream - 50 ml
- Salt according to taste
- Cottage cheese - 1 tbsp
- Egg - 1

Instructions

Beat eggs with cottage cheese, baking powder, and powder from a bag with KetoDiet omelet. Pour the resulting dough into a decorating bag and make speckles into boiling salted water— Cook for about 3 minutes. Pour the cooked specks and fry dry until golden in a hot pan.

Place the finished speckles on a plate and fry the finely chopped onion, garlic in the pan and fry for a while. Return the speckle to the pan, mix, pour over the cream, mix in the baby spinach and finally sprinkle with grated Parmesan cheese.

5. Keto Mushrooms with Celery Fries

Servings: 1 **Preparation:** 40 minutes
Ingredients
- Herbs for decoration
- Celery - 200 g
- KetoDiet Protein omelet with bacon flavor - 1 serving
- Olive oil - 2 tbsp
- Pepper according to taste
- Salt according to taste
- Water - 100 ml
- Mushrooms - 3 pcs

Instructions
Clean the celery, cut it into thin fries, drizzle with olive oil, salt, pepper, and bake in the oven for about 15 minutes at 165 ° C. We watch the french fries in the oven because it depends on how strong we cut them. Meanwhile, cut the mushrooms into slices and mix them with the protein omelet mixed in water. The mushrooms wrapped "in batter" from an omelet are then sautéed until golden in oil. We can pour the rest of the omelet on the mushroom pan so that we don't miss a bit of protein. Serve with celery fries.

6. Turkey Roll with Spring Onion, Olives, and Sun-Dried tomatoes

Servings: 4 **Preparation time:** 80 minutes
Ingredients
- Balsamic to taste
- Black olives - 60 g
- Garlic - 20 g

- Cherry tomatoes - 280 g
- Spring onion - 120 g
- Turkey breast - 400 g
- Olive oil - 40 ml
- Pepper to taste
- Rocket - 120 g
- Salt to taste
- Dried tomatoes in oil - 60 g

Instructions

Carefully cut the turkey breast lengthwise so that a larger pancake is formed and tap the meat. Fry the finely chopped spring onion and garlic. Add olives cut in half and sliced sun-dried tomatoes, and fry everything briefly. Apply the mixture to a slice of turkey meat and carefully roll it into a roll. Tie with thread and bake at 180 degrees for 50 minutes. Cut the finished roll into slices and serve with arugula salad and fresh cherry tomatoes flavored with olive oil and balsamic.

7. Zucchini Lasagna

Servings: 2 **Preparation time:** 60 minutes

Ingredients

- Basil as required
- Red wine - 1 glass
- Onion - 1
- Zucchini - 1
- Ground beef - 250 g
- Olive oil as required
- Pepper to taste
- Tomatoes - 1 can (without added sugar)
- Whipping cream - 1 piece
- Grated cheddar to taste
- Salt to taste
- Egg - 1 piece

Instructions
Fry the diced onion, add the minced meat, salt, pepper, add basil and sauté. Once the meat has pulled, cover with red wine and stew. When the wine boils, add chopped tomatoes, cover, and simmer for about 30 minutes. Cut the zucchini lengthwise into thin slices. It works best with a potato peeler, but we can also playfully handle it with a knife. Wipe the baking dish with butter, layout the zucchini slices, pour the sauce over the minced meat, sprinkle with grated cheddar, and pour over the beaten egg in the cream. Layer another layer of zucchini, sauce, cheddar, and pour again with cream and egg. We repeat the whole thing, and we finish with a layer of cheddar and cream. Bake in a preheated oven at 200 degrees for about 30 minutes.

8. Keto Soup with Zucchini
Servings: 1 **Preparations:** 15 minutes
Ingredients
- Herbs according to taste
- Garlic - 1 clove
- Onion - 1/2 pcs
- Zucchini - 150 g
- KetoDiet protein cheese soup with vegetables - 1 piece
- Butter - 1 teaspoon
- Olive oil - 20 ml
- Pepper according to taste
- Water - 250 ml

Instructions
In a small saucepan, fry the zucchini chopped in olive oil, add salt, pepper, herbs, and garlic. Pour water and cook until soft. Finally, stir in the cheese protein soup, a teaspoon of butter, turn off the flame and let it run for 3 minutes. Garnish with herbs.

9. Pumpkin with Greek Feta Cheese
Servings: 2 **Preparation time:** 85 minutes
Ingredients
- Hokaido pumpkins - 1
- Olive oil as required
- Pepper to taste
- Sunflower seeds to taste
- Garlic cloves - 3
- Salt to taste
- Feta cheese - 100 g
- Thyme - 2 sprigs
- Walnuts as required

Instructions
Peel the pumpkin, remove the seeds, cut into larger cubes, and spread in a baking dish.

We don't peel garlic, so let's avoid burning it. Bake the mixture for about 40 minutes at 180 degrees, then add the walnuts and sunflower seeds and bake gently for about 10 minutes. We do not add nuts sooner so that they do not burn. Take the baked goods out of the oven and sprinkle with grated feta cheese. To make the cheese beautifully baked, put it in the oven for another 5 minutes.

10. Keto Houstičky with Herb Butter

Serving: 3 **Preparation time:** 60 minutes
Ingredients

7. White - 3 pcs
8. Herbs to taste (for herb butter)
9. Pumpkin seeds - 1 tbsp
10. Hot water - 1/2 cup
11. Apple vinegar - 2 teaspoons
12. KetoDiet Protein Drink - 2 servings
13. Baking powder - 2 teaspoons
14. Gourmet yeast - 2 tablespoons
15. Almond flour - 1 and 1/4 cup
16. Butter - 4 tablespoons (for herb butter)
17. Psyllium (fiber) - 5 tablespoons
18. Sunflower or flax seeds - 1 tbsp
19. Salt - 1 teaspoon
20. Maldon saltfor sprinkling
21. Yolk - 1 piece

Instructions

Mix the ingredients, including the protein powder, and add hot water while whipping constantly. Add a pinch of salt, stir again. We shape 6 buns from the dough and place on a baking sheet. We leave gaps between them, because the pastry will increase in volume during baking. Brush the buns with egg yolk and bake for about 30 minutes at 160 ° C. Let the finished buns cool down and serve them with herb butter, for example, which we prepare by mixing herbs according to your taste into the softened butter and letting them harden to any shape in the fridge. We used parsley, basil, and thyme.

11. Baked Keto Fennel

Servings: 2 **Preparation time:** 70 minutes
Ingredients

- Fresh fennel - 2 bulbs
- Pumpkin seeds - 2 tablespoons
- KetoDiet protein omelet with cheese flavor - 1 serving
- Olive oil - 1 tablespoon
- Chive
- Pepper

- Parsley
- Sunflower seeds - 2 tablespoons
- Whipping cream - 150 ml
- Salt according to taste
- Hard cheese - 50 g

Instructions

Wash and cut the fennel into slices, which we place in a baking dish. Season with salt, pepper, herbs, and mix with olive oil. Pour in a protein omelet mixed in cream, cover with grated cheese and bake at 165 ° C for about 50 minutes. Meanwhile, fry the pumpkin and sunflower seeds dry in a pan and sprinkle them on the finished meal. Garnish with, for example, the remaining herbs or sprigs of fennel.

12. Wholemeal Couscous with Cherry Tomatoes

Serving: 1 **Preparation time:** 20 minutes

Ingredients

- Wholegrain couscous - 50 g
- Fresh basil handful
- Garlic - 1 clove
- Cherry tomatoes - 5 pcs
- Half Zucchini
- KetoDiet chicken/beef protein soup (depends on your taste)1 bag
- Olive oil - 1 tbsp
- Parmesan - 30 g
- Sunflower seeds - 2 spoons for pesto + 1 spoon for decoration
- Water - 100 ml

Instructions

Prepare the protein soup in 100 ml of water and let it stand for 3 minutes. Pour the finished soup over the dry couscous and let stand for another 5 minutes to soak up the couscous. Meanwhile, cut the zucchini into rounds, fry it dry on both sides, add olive oil, tomatoes, and garlic and fry the mixture. Add the finished couscous, a spoonful of pesto, and mix. Garnish with fresh basil, a little pesto, and roasted sunflower seeds and serve. How to make homemade basil pesto? Very simple! We mix a handful of basil, 2 tablespoons of sunflower seeds, 2 tablespoons of olive oil, and 2 tablespoons of grated Parmesan cheese and decorate the finished couscous with it.

Dinner

1. Keto Pasta with Zucchini

Servings: 1 **Preparation time:** 20 minutes
Ingredients

- Fresh parsley according to taste
- Garlic - 1 clove
- Zucchini - 120 g
- Pumpkin seeds - 1 tbsp
- KetoDiet protein pasta Fusilli - 1 piece
- Olive oil - 1 tbsp
- Salt according to taste
- The egg white - 1 piece

Instructions

Cut the zucchini into pieces. Fry the pumpkin seeds dry in a pan. Pour the seeds into a bowl and fry finely chopped or pressed garlic in oil and add the zucchini. Once the zucchini softens, add the cooked protein pasta according to the instructions and pour over the protein. Salt and mix until the pasta is slightly combined with the zucchini and the egg whites. Finally, sprinkle with fried pumpkin seeds and garnish with parsley.

2. Keto Pizza

Servings: 1 serving **Preparation time:** 60 minutes
Ingredients

4. Broccoli - 250 g
5. Fresh baby spinach handful (for lining)
6. Garlic - 1 clove (for lining)
7. KetoDiet Protein Drink - 1 scoop (15 g)
8. Oregano to taste (for dough and lining)
9. Parmesan - 10 g
10. Parmesan for sprinkling
11. Pepper
12. Tomatoes - 2 pcs (for lining)
13. Egg - 1 piece
14. Mushrooms - 2 pcs (for lining)

Instructions

We break down the broccoli into roses, which we mix in a small mixer. Spread the broccoli on a baking sheet lined and bake for 10 minutes in an oven preheated to 180 ° C. Mix baked broccoli with egg, protein drink, and grated parmesan, salt, and pepper. Make a pancake from the dough, spread a mixture of mixed tomatoes, garlic, and oregano on it.

Put with sliced mushrooms and lightly sprinkle with grated Parmesan cheese. Bake the pizza at 180 ° C for about 15 minutes. Garnish with baby spinach before serving.

3. Baked Portobello Mushrooms

Servings: 4 **Preparation time:** 30 minutes
Ingredients
- Red onion - 1
- Garlic according to taste
- Cherry tomatoes - 4
- Goat cheese - 150 g
- Ground beef - 250 g
- Pepper
- Vegetable oil
- Salt
- Thyme
- Portobello mushroom - 4

Instructions
We clean the heads of mushrooms, remove the foot and hollow out the inside, cut the foot into smaller pieces. Heat oil in a pan and add minced meat, thyme, crushed garlic, salt, pepper, and sauté for a while. Add the inside of the mushroom and a sliced leg to the meat. Fill the finished mixture with mushroom caps, place the sliced red onion, sliced cherry tomatoes on the wheels, and sprinkle with grated cheese. Bake for 25 minutes in an oven heated to 180 ° C. Mushrooms are served with fresh vegetable salad.

4. Baked Protein Omelette

Serving: 1 **Preparation time:** 30 minutes
Ingredients
- Cherry tomatoes - 2
- Zucchini - 50 g
- KetoDiet cheese omelette - 1
- Chard - 20 g
- Pepper
- Vegetable oil
- Salt
- Hard cheese (up to 30% fat in dry matter) - 50 g
- Mushrooms - 50 g

Instructions
Cut the zucchini into pieces, slice the mushrooms, salt, pepper and fry together for a while in hot oil; add the sliced chard leaf, mix and put in a baking dish. In the shaker, mix the protein omelet according to the instructions and pour on the mixture.

Add chopped cherry tomatoes and sprinkle with grated cheese—Bake for about 25 minutes at 180 ° C.

5. Zucchini Pie

Servings: 4
Preparation time: 60 minutes
Ingredients
- Basil to taste
- Zucchini - 1
- Mozzarella - 1
- Pepper to taste
- Salt to taste
- Egg - 3

Instructions
In a bowl, mix 1 larger mozzarella with 3 eggs. Grate the zucchini, mix everything, salt, and pepper. Pour into a baking dish. Garnish the slices of tomato on top, we can also add fresh basil leaves. Bake at a temperature of 180 degrees for about 30-40 minutes.

6. Salad with Olives and Cottage Cheese

Serving: 1 **Preparation time:** 15 minutes
Ingredients
1. Black olives as required
2. Cucumber salad - 1/2
3. Pepper - 1
4. Pepper to taste
5. Tomatoes - 2
6. Salt to taste
7. Cottage cheese - 1

Instructions

Cut the vegetables into cubes, add the black olives to taste, salt, pepper, and mix with 1 cup of cottage cheese. Sprinkle with finely chopped chives on top.

7. Vegetable Salad with Goat Cheese

Servings: 2 **Preparation time:** 30 minutes
Ingredients
- Balsamic - 1 tablespoon
- Cherry tomatoes as required
- Goat cheese - 2 slices
- Olive oil - 2 tablespoons + for dripping
- Seed mixture (sunflower, pumpkin) - 1 package
- A mixture of green salads (arugula, romaine lettuce, corn salad) - 1 package

Instructions
Cut goat cheese into thicker slices and grill or fry dry in a non-stick pan. Mix popular types of green salads with cherry tomatoes and season with a mixture of olive oil and balsamic. We can taste it with a pinch of salt and, depending on the taste, also pepper. Place the roasted goat cheese slices on a salad, sprinkle with a mixture of seeds and drizzle with olive oil.

Desserts

1. Keto Panna Cotta with Wild Berries

Servings: 1 **Preparation time:** 80 minutes
Ingredients
- Forest fruit - 100 g
- Milk - 100 ml
- Protein panna cotta with cream and vanilla flavor - 1 bag

Instructions

According to the instructions, mix the protein panna cotta in milk, pour it into a mold, and let it solidify in the refrigerator. Pour the finished panna cotta onto a plate and garnish with mixed forest fruits and a sprig of mint.

2. Sweet Potato-Pumpkin Christmas Salad

Servings: 4 **Preparation time:** 60 minutes
Ingredients
- Sweet potatoes - 2 pieces
- Chili spice pinch if you like spicy dishes
- Spring onion one volume
- Gherkin, according to taste
- A smaller butter pumpkin or a smaller Hokaido pumpkin1 piece
- Pepper according to taste
- Whole mustard - 3 tbsp
- Salt according to taste
- Egg - 4 pieces

Instructions
Cut the pumpkin, carve it out and cut into the same smaller cubes. We also peel and dice sweet potatoes into cubes (we select larger pieces). We cook everything in salted water for about 10 minutes. Drain the water and let it cool completely. Meanwhile, we boil the eggs hard, peel them, and cut them into cubes. We also finely chop pickles and spring onions. We definitely do not miss it; it will give the salad a great taste. Mix everything, salt, pepper, season with mustard, and mayonnaise. The salad will be better if we let it cool down and rest a little.

3. Unbaked Cheesecake in a glass

Servings: 8 **Preparation time:** 20 minutes
Ingredients
- chicory syrup to taste
- Mascarpone - 1
- Blackberries for decoration
- Whipped cream - 1 (whipped)
- Philadelphia cheese - 1 package

Instructions
Carefully mix the cheese and whipped cream with chicory syrup and pour into the prepared glasses. Garnish with blueberries or strawberries. Let cool in the fridge for at least an hour.

4. Chocolate Muesli Balls with Nuts

Servings: 15 **Preparation:** 30 minutes
Ingredients
- 70% dark chocolate - 25 g
- Fine muesli KetoLife - 150 g
- Hazelnuts - 30 g
- Butter - 70 g
- Protein cream with hazelnuts - 100 g

Instructions
From fine muesli, protein cream with hazelnuts (we use either 2 smaller packages of cream or 5 tablespoons from a large package), and melted butter, we create a dough from which we form balls. Put 1 hazelnut in each and wrap in melted 70% chocolate and chopped hazelnuts. We store the balls in the refrigerator.

5. Sweet Potato Muffins

Servings: 3 **Preparation time:** 50 minutes
Ingredients
- Sweet potatoes - 250 g
- Blueberries handful
- Chicory syrup to taste
- KetoDiet protein mixture - 2 measuring cups
- Baking powder - 1 bag
- Almond flour - 25 g
- Cinnamon - 1 tbsp
- Egg - 4
- Walnuts - 2 tablespoons (ground)

Instructions
Thoroughly mix the grated muffins with other ingredients, or mix and pour into molds (6 pcs). Bake at 180 degrees for 15-20 minutes.

6. Walnut-Chocolate Balls

Servings: 12 **Preparation time:** 30 minutes
Ingredients
- Chicory syrup according to taste
- Hot chocolate - 100 g
- Cocoa for wrapping
- Coconut for wrapping
- Butter according to need
- Rum aroma according to taste
- Cinnamon for wrapping
- Walnuts - 250 g

Instructions
For 50 balls. Grind the nuts, mix with melted chocolate, butter, rum aroma, syrup. We make balls from the dough, which we wrap in cinnamon, cocoa, or coconut.

7. Chocolate Laundries

Servings: 5 **Preparation time:** 45 minutes
Ingredients
- Birch sugar xylitol - 3 tablespoons
- Cocoa - 3 tablespoons
- Baking powder - 1 teaspoon
- Almond flour - 70 g
- Butter - 35 g
- Dried whey - 20 g
- Egg yolk - 2

Instructions
We mix all the ingredients and work out the dough with our hands, which we press into the laundries' molds—Bake in the oven at 180 ° C for about 8 minutes.

8. Coconuts in Chocolate

Servings: 12 **Preparation time:** 45 minutes
Ingredients
- Hot chocolate according to need
- Whole cottage cheese8 tablespoons
- Shredded coconut - 200 g
- The egg white - 4

Instructions
We whip the snow from the proteins. Mix the ingredients in a bowl and use a spoon to form balls, which we bake on baking paper at a temperature of 160 ° C until golden. Soak in melted chocolate.

9. Linen Wheels

Servings: 6
Preparation time: 45 minutes
Ingredients
- Chicory syrup - 3 tablespoons
- Baking powder - 1 teaspoon
- Almond flour - 70 g
- Butter - 35 g
- Dried whey - 20 g
- Egg yolk - 2 pcs

Instructions
From these ingredients, we make a dough, which we leave to rest in the fridge for several hours. Then roll out on a thin pancake and cut out the wheels or hearts as you wish. Bake on baking paper at 170 ° C for about 10 minutes. After cooling, combine with jam or chocolate cream without sugar.

10. Almond Balls

Servings: 4 **Preparation time:** 50 minutes
Ingredients
- Cocoa - 2 tablespoons
- KetoDiet Protein Drink - 2 tablespoons
- Almond flour - 3 tablespoons
- Almond butter - 3 tablespoons
- Shredded coconut - 2 tablespoons

Instructions
Mix almond butter, ground nuts, grated coconut, cocoa powder, and a chocolate-flavored protein drink and work everything into the dough. Divide into 12 equal parts, from which we form balls. We then wrap the individual balls in coconut and cocoa powder.

CHAPTER 5

30-Day Meal Plan

Week 1

Day One
Breakfast: Chorizo Breakfast Bake
Lunch: Sesame Pork Lettuce Wraps
Dinner: Avocado Lime Salmon

Day Two
Breakfast: Keto Potato Pancakes
Lunch: Keto Pasta Curry
Dinner: Leftover Avocado Lime Salmon

Day Three
Breakfast: Baked Eggs in Avocado
Lunch: Easy Beef Curry
Dinner: Veggies and Rosemary Roasted Chicken

Day Four
Breakfast: Lemon Poppy Ricotta Pancakes with 3 Slices Thick-Cut Bacon
Lunch: Zucchini lasagna
Dinner: Leftover Rosemary Roasted Chicken and Veggies

Day Five
Breakfast: Leftover Lemon Poppy Ricotta Pancakes with 3 Slices Thick-Cut Bacon
Lunch: Keto Pasta Curry
Dinner: Cheesy Sausage Mushroom Skillet with 1 Slice Thick-Cut Bacon

Day Six
Breakfast: Sweet Blueberry Coconut Porridge with 1 Slice Thick-Cut Bacon
Lunch: Avocado foam
Dinner: Baked portobello mushrooms

Day Seven
Breakfast: Leftover Sweet Blueberry Coconut Porridge
Lunch: Keto soup with zucchini
Dinner: Keto Pasta with Zucchini

Week 2

Day One
Breakfast: Banana Keto Chia Pudding
Lunch: Easy Cheeseburger Salad
Dinner: Chicken Zoodle Alfredo

Day Two
Breakfast: Savory Ham and Cheese Waffles with 2 Slices Thick-Cut Bacon
Lunch: Keto Pasta Curry
Dinner: Cabbage and Sausage Skillet

Day Three
Breakfast: Keto Potato Pancakes
Lunch: Pumpkin with Greek feta cheese
Dinner: Baked portobello mushrooms

Day Four
Breakfast: Keto Waffles with Chocolate Cottage Cheese
Lunch: Avocado foam
Dinner: Zucchini pie

Day Five
Breakfast: Keto Potato Pancakes
Lunch: Sausage Skillet and Cabbage
Dinner: Keto Pasta with Zucchini

Day Six
Breakfast: Matcha Keto Pudding
Lunch: Vegetable-mushroom Keto Omelette
Dinner: Zucchini pie

Day Seven
Breakfast: Keto Tart with wild berries
Lunch: Pumpkin with Greek feta cheese
Dinner: Salad with olives and Cottage cheese

Week 3

Day One
Breakfast: Green Keto Smoothie
Lunch: Mozzarella Tuna Melt
Dinner: Cheesy Single-Serve Lasagna

Day Two
Breakfast: Bacon Breakfast Bombs
Lunch: Avocado, Salami Sandwiches, and Egg
Dinner: Crispy Chipotle Chicken Thighs

Day Three
Breakfast: Keto Waffles with Chocolate Cottage Cheese
Lunch: Keto Pasta Curry
Dinner: Ham, Pepperoni, and Cheese Stromboli

Day Four
Breakfast: Matcha Keto Pudding
Lunch: Avocado foam
Dinner: Cheese Stromboli, Leftover Pepperoni and Ham

Day Five
Breakfast: Keto Tart with wild berries
Lunch: Keto Pasta Curry
Dinner: Keto Pasta with Zucchini

Day Six
Breakfast: Three-Cheese Pizza Frittata with 2 Slices Thick-Cut Bacon
Lunch: Keto Pasta Curry
Dinner: Spring Salad with Steak and Sweet Dressing

Day Seven
Breakfast: Leftover Three-Cheese Pizza Frittata with 2 Slices Thick-Cut Bacon
Lunch: Vegetable-mushroom Keto Omelette
Dinner: Keto Pasta with Zucchini

Week 4

Day One
Breakfast: Keto Tart with wild berries
Lunch: Zucchini Pasta Salad and Chicken
Dinner: *Carb Up* Flank Steak, Watermelon Salad, and Plantains
Snacks: Mojito Water

Day Two
Breakfast: Keto Tart with wild berries
Lunch: Keto Mushrooms with celery fries
Dinner: Chicken and Bacon with Slaw
Snacks: Tropical Coconut Balls

Day Three
Breakfast: Baked Keto Peppers
Lunch: Sardine Salad
Dinner: Chorizo Bowl
Snacks: Jicama Fries

Day Four
Breakfast: Rocket Fuel Latte with Maca
Lunch: Zucchini Pasta Salad and Chicken
Dinner: Keto Pasta with Zucchini
Snacks: Mojito Water

Day Five
Breakfast: Pasta Salad
Lunch: Vanilla Creme Gummies
Dinner: Salad with olives and Cottage cheese
Snacks: Jicama Fries

Day Six
Breakfast: Veggie Frittata
Lunch: Sardine Salad
Dinner: Chicken and Bacon with Slaw
Snacks: Tropical Coconut Balls

Day Seven
Breakfast: Baked Keto Peppers
Lunch: Chicken and Zucchini Pasta Salad
Dinner: Keto Pasta with Zucchini
Snacks: Mojito Water

Week 5

Day One
Breakfast: Mozzarella Veggie-Loaded Quiche with 1 Slice Thick-Cut Bacon
Lunch: Keto Pasta Curry
Dinner: Salad with olives and Cottage cheese

Day Two
Breakfast: Keto Tart with wild berries
Lunch: Vegetable-mushroom Keto Omelette
Dinner: Keto Pasta with Zucchini

CONCLUSION

The ketogenic diet can offer benefits to women during menopause, including increased sensitivity to insulin, decreased weight gain, and decreased cravings.

It can, however, increase some cardiovascular disease risk factors and reduce the intake of many essential nutrients. What's more, during your body's transition to ketosis, keto flu can temporarily exacerbate the symptoms of menopause.

While the ketogenic diet can work during menopause for some women, bear in mind that it is not a one-size-fits-all solution for everyone.

It's a wise idea to consider other less restrictive ways to improve your health and meet your fitness goals before trying out the keto diet.

Printed in Great Britain
by Amazon

25656340R00084